TOM GRAVENEY AT LORD'S

A Year at the Home of Cricket

Stephen Fay

Illustrations by Karen Neale

Best wishes, Simon

Tom Graveney

Mar 05

To Simon O'Hagan, who allowed me to become a cricket writer, and who is, therefore, responsible for Methuen *this book.*

love Stephen

Published in 2005
by Methuen in association with
Marylebone Cricket Club

10 9 8 7 6 5 4 3 2 1

Methuen & Co. Limited
11–12 Buckingham Gate, London SW1E 6LB
Registered number 5278590

Marylebone Cricket Club
Lord's Ground, London NW8 8QN

A CIP catalogue record for this book
is available from the British Library

ISBN 0 413 77530 5

Illustrations and captions © Karen Neale

Designed by Bryony Newhouse

Printed and bound in Great Britain by The Bath Press

CONTENTS

FOREWORD

All institutions change, some more quickly than others. Some enjoy it; some resist it, and by doing so, write a first draft of their obituary. Some are more conscious of change than others, and among those is the Marylebone Cricket Club. MCC can hardly fail to be conscious of the changes that have occurred at Lord's in the past 20 years. All they need do is look around them. A ground that encapsulated history and authority in cricket had become dowdy and uncomfortable. In the past 20 years, Lord's has been transformed into an architectural showcase. Spectators can sit and watch in comfort; they can also get a good cup of coffee and a decent bacon roll. The mindset has changed, too. MCC was a members' club that prided itself on its exclusivity. I think of that as Old Lord's. The New Lord's is more open and accommodating; more conscious of the requirements of paying spectators, though not at the expense of the members' privileges. (I should perhaps declare an interest: I am a member of MCC.)

The way institutions work, and how they deal with change, has long been an interest of mine. When I wrote about the Bank of England 20 years ago, it was in the middle of a radical upheaval. I found that the people who worked there were interested in what was happening to them, and happy to discuss it. This was true of MCC, too. If my story sometimes seems short on cricket, this is because I was given the opportunity to talk the people who run every facet of MCC and of Lord's. I was allowed to sit in on committee meetings, and to talk freely to committee members, to the management, and the workers. I am grateful to Charles Fry, the chairman, Roger Knight, the Secretary and Chief Executive, and Colin Maynard, the assistant secretary, for their support for the project. Naturally, I am grateful to all the members and employees of MCC who spoke to me; their names are recorded in the text. I received encouragement from the Publishing sub-committee of the Arts and Library Committee, and its chairman, Dr Gerald Howat. Adam Chadwick, the energetic curator, got me going. Sally Goldfield, Glenys Roberts and Ken Daldry in the library helped keep me going.

I must single out Tom Graveney. Without his enthusiasm for the idea, his generosity with his time, and his willingness to share his experience, this book could not have taken its present form. I am grateful to him for being delightful company.

Stephen Fay
OCTOBER, 2005

THE CHOICE

Tom Graveney's selection as President of Marylebone Cricket Club was extraordinary. Fifty years ago the Presidency of MCC was a job for the grandest of establishment grandees. In the 1950s there had been two Dukes, two Viscounts, one Earl, one Field Marshal, one Marshal of the RAF, one Knight and just two plain commoners. The Duke of Edinburgh was President twice and his presence reflected MCC's image of itself. It was a gentlemen's club, run by dedicated committee men who did it for the love of the game, and deplored interference, even from the President, no matter how grand he was. The idea that a professional cricketer might be considered for the job was never entertained. Cricketers were not blackballed. On the contrary, since 1949 the best had been awarded honorary memberships. Graveney himself had become an honorary life member in 1972 shortly after his retirement. By the 1980s, the inner circle was being widened to include some of the best amateur cricketers: Peter May and Colin Cowdrey were succeeded in the 1990s by Tony Lewis and Ted Dexter, all England captains. But no professional cricketer had ever been invited to be President.

The hierarchy at MCC is puzzling. Besides a President there is a Chairman, who is chosen by the MCC Committee from a shortlist produced by the club's trustees. But the next President is chosen by the incumbent President. In the year starting on 1 October 2003, the President was from a family that belongs among the aristocracy of cricket. Charles Fry is the grandson of C. B. Fry, a cricketing legend a hundred years ago. At the end

1

of his term in September 2004 he became Chairman of MCC, succeeding Lord Alexander, the recently retired lawyer and banker and one of the principal architects of significant changes at MCC.

Fry is tall and well built; he had played cricket at Oxford which put him in touch with the fringes of the first-class game, and he stood for the MCC Committee in the 1980s as a reformer because he believed that Lord's in the mid-1980s was burdened by a sclerotic administration: 'the whole of Lord's was disintegrating,' he says. He is an active and talkative Chairman, and when he is not at Lord's, he is to be found in a smart suite of offices of a property development company in Cavendish Square, which are decorated throughout with photographs and paintings of cricketers, including his grandfather.

The Chairmanship put Fry at the centre of MCC's web of committees. At the start of the new millennium, changes in the internal balance of power meant that the Chairman had become more influential than the President. The Presidency had been retained, but the role had changed. Now he was no longer required to immerse himself in the management of MCC. The job, as titular head of MCC, was to focus on representing the club in public. The changes made the appointment of Tom Graveney both possible and plausible.

While he was still President early in 2004, Charles Fry was contemplating a list of potential successors. He is expected to listen to the advice of predecessors such as Sir Tim Rice, the cricket-mad songwriter, who had chosen him, he talked to friends on the MCC Committee, and to Roger Knight, but the final decision rests with him alone. 'It's the most difficult decision any President has to take,' says Fry. The consensus was that the next President ought to be a cricketer. Names surfaced – M. J. K. Smith, who had retired from the chairmanship of Warwickshire; Doug Insole and Micky Stewart. But Fry suddenly had another idea.

One perk of the Presidency is a winter break in the sun watching England on tour. In the winter of 2002/03, this pleasure must have seemed more of a duty. Although MCC is no longer the governing body of world cricket, and its formal authority is limited to making and interpreting the Laws of cricket, the idea that Lord's is the home of cricket remains strong. This meant the presence of MCC's President was required to celebrate England's first-ever Test in Bangladesh, the newest Test-playing nation.

During a detour in India on the way, Fry ran into Tom Graveney, who was travelling with his wife Jackie. They had met when Fry played as an Oxford undergraduate against Graveney's Worcestershire team, and they had seen each other over the years when Graveney was entertaining guests in one of the Mound Stand boxes at Lord's. But the first occasion when they spent time together was in the sub-continent in the winter of 2003. Fry had always been impressed by Graveney's batting – 'a wonderful cricketer in his time' – but now he warmed to the private person. 'He's such a perfect gentleman. A lovely man.' It occurred to him then that Graveney would be a good candidate for the Presidency, especially as the Australians would be touring during the 2005 season, and Graveney had played in six Ashes series.

The final decision has to be made before MCC's annual general meeting in May, and by February Fry was still not absolutely certain. Graveney looked well and seemed fit, but he was 77 and Fry needed to know whether he thought he was strong enough to survive a gruelling social schedule. Tim Rice mentioned that he knew Tim Graveney, Tom's son, and volunteered to ask him about his father's state of health. What happened next was not in the script. Tim Graveney interpreted Tim Rice's query as an invitation. He told his father that he had heard a rumour that Tom was to be asked to President of MCC. 'Don't take the mickey out of your father,' Tom replied. But this conversation pre-empted any change of heart on Charles Fry's part. The leak had made up his mind for him. 'It was a bit of a mistake,' he says, but it was a decision he had no cause to regret.

Graveney's membership of MCC was honorary. He had no experience of running a sizeable organisation. 'In the sense that he had not been involved in the club at all, Tom is the least political of MCC presidents,' says Roger Knight, MCC's Secretary and Chief Executive. But experience was not relevant. Fry explains: 'The President doesn't have to know how to run the club. I don't think he should interfere with what is going on.' Graveney appreciates that the President is a figurehead. But he is a particularly conspicuous one.

Although Graveney was let into the secret earlier than he intended, Fry kept it very quiet at Lord's. In retrospect, he did drop one clue at a committee meeting when he said he didn't think cricket had been particularly kind to Tom Graveney, but no one seemed to pick it up. Knight sensed that the appointment of a former professional would be a symbol of a new style at MCC, but in the press announcement no mention was made of Graveney being the first former professional cricketer to be appointed President. The initial public response was surprise. Because the motive was not obvious to people outside Lord's, some assumed that this was a public relations gimmick designed as part of MCC's conscious attempt to improve its image. Not so, says Fry. 'I never saw it as a public relations exercise,' he says. 'I saw Tom as a man who I would be proud to have as President of MCC.'

TOM GRAVENEY: ELEGANT REBEL

The President of Marylebone Cricket Club makes his debut at the first meeting of the Executive Board after 1 October, when his one-year term officially starts. He will spend many hours in committee meetings before the year is out. Even though they have the turnover of medium-sized companies, clubs like MCC differ from public companies with streamlined managements because, instead of shareholders, they have members who elect representatives to the MCC Committee. None of the participants would claim that the system is efficient, but the Executive Board is an attempt to make it more so. Senior members of the staff and selected committee chairmen make decisions about how Lord's is run, and, as if to show how earnest they are, the meetings start at 8.30 a.m.

The Executive Board normally meets in the Committee Room on the ground floor of the Pavilion, but in October 2004 cricket's most iconic building was shrouded in plastic sheeting. An extensive and expensive refurbishment of the Pavilion began as soon as the cricket had stopped. On 5 October 2004 the Executive Board was meeting on the first floor of the Warner Stand. Roger Knight brought the Board up to date on the intentions of the ICC, which seemed determined to leave its headquarters at Lord's for Dubai; there was an update on MCC's plans to take over a major part of university cricket; England's controversial and unhappy tour of Zimbabwe was also on the agenda. But the first item was to welcome MCC's new President.

Tom Graveney has the bearing of a man who was once a fine sportsman: around six feet tall, standing straight. He had both hips replaced and a heart bypass a few years ago and gets a check-up before he flies; otherwise he shows no deference to his age. Len Hutton once observed: 'He's got a red face,' before adding: 'I don't like red faces.' Graveney still has a red face. He also has an easygoing nature, an engaging smile, a flow of stories about cricket and a remarkable memory for past players and the matches they played together.

To Southerners, Graveney is a West Countryman. To Northerners, he is a Southerner. In fact, he was born in the North, in Newcastle on 16 June 1927. His mother remarried when his father died and moved south, via Blackpool, to Bristol. When he completed a good grammar school

THE PAVILION ROOF TERRACE BEFORE REFURBISHMENT: '*Saturday September 4th and September 5th 2004 – summer has returned and literally an Indian summer for the two international one-day matches between Australia and Pakistan on Saturday and especially England and India on Sunday. This match enjoyed a capacity crowd of about 30,000 and at least half of that seemed to be a wave of pale blue around the ground of very enthusiastic and vocal Indian supporters, who weren't disappointed…*'

education at seventeen and a half he joined the Army while there was still a war on. At cricket, he was a precocious talent. He learned to pick the bat up straight and keep his head still. After that, he says, all you have to do is pick the length, and no coach can do that for you. At school he had not considered cricket as a career. Fewer than five years later he was twelfth man in the Gloucestershire side when the 1948 Australian Invincibles scored 783 for 6 at Nevil Road in Bristol.

The reason Graveney is a legend is not because of the number of runs he scored, although there were plenty of them – 47,793 first-class runs and 122 hundreds – but because of the way he made them. He was the great stylist of his generation who left a powerful visual image of a batsman leaning elegantly on the front foot and placing the ball precisely where he wished it to go. He cannot explain how he did it. He was not much coached. 'It just happened that way. It's what's given to you,' he says. This fatalism, linked to a laid-back attitude, was a strength and a weakness. 'Being stylish is lovely when you're going well, but when you're in a bad patch, you lose your middle stump and everyone calls it a casual shot.' Nonetheless, Graveney was the subject of one of Neville Cardus's more extravagant assessments: 'If some destructive process were to eliminate all we know about cricket, with only Graveney remaining, we could reconstruct from him every outline of the game . . . every essential character and flavour contributing to cricket,' he wrote.

Graveney fondly remembers the time he spent in the middle at Lord's. He has every reason to, having scored 843 runs at an average of 56.20 in eleven Tests, the first in 1952 and the last in 1968. He made two of his eleven Test hundreds at Lord's, but he was frankly disappointed by his first visit in 1949, aged 22. In a rare lapse of memory, he thought he had played for Gloucestershire against Middlesex: in fact, it was for the Players against the Gentlemen, in only his second season in first-class cricket. In an inauspicious debut, he was out for 2 and 5, which may explain why the match was so forgettable. What he does remember vividly is looking out of a Long Room window, and thinking how odd it was that the ground was not flat. He had not expected such a pronounced slope from Grand Stand to Tavern. He also noted that there was no sight screen at the Pavilion End. 'You'd lose the ball a bit in the windows,' he recalls. But members insisted on an uninterrupted view and the players lacked the clout to overrule them.

He was then not long out of the Army. He had held the rank of Captain and had been stationed in Suez, where he acted as depot sports officer in a training camp: 'Played sport every day. Great fun.' Such fun that Graveney decided to make a career of the Army. However, when he was on leave in 1947, his brother Ken, himself a fine cricketer for Gloucestershire until he was disabled by a bad back, arranged for him to play in the county team in a couple of benefit games. Charlie Barnett, an England player before the war who now captained the county, had been particularly impressed by one double-century and told Graveney that, if he decided to quit the Army, there would be a job for him with Gloucestershire.

His first season started disastrously, but Barnett persevered and the 1949 *Wisden* reported: 'A pleasant feature [of the 1948 season] was the form of a newcomer, T. W. Graveney, a 21-year-old product of Bristol club cricket, who showed graceful right-handed stroke play.' He scored his first hundred that year, and in only his fourth season he was selected for England, and played against India in his first Lord's Test in 1952, when he opened his account with 73. He performed just well enough to play in all five Tests against Australia in the halcyon year of 1953, when England regained the Ashes. But in the early years, the promise was unfulfilled. Watching Graveney's 111 at Sydney in 1954/55, Alan Ross wrote that 'he played like the batsman one had always hoped he would become.' Len Hutton, England's first professional captain, had become impatient: 'I'm a bit afraid that he is not quite the chap for the big occasion when the heat is on,' he told Geoffrey Howard, who managed that tour to Australia. Hutton's more measured judgement was that there was nothing wrong with Graveney's ability: 'All Tom lacked was confidence,' he said.

Graveney enjoyed cricket and cricketers. There was mutual trust ('If you nicked the ball, you walked'), and the professionals got on well ('There were few people you didn't like. We used to enjoy playing against each other'). Few were in it for the money. Graveney had been a Test cricketer for four years before he could finally afford a Ford Anglia. 'The game was different then. We played our cricket hard. We made sure we were fit enough to play the following day, but we still enjoyed our half-dozen pints in the evening. In those days cricket writers wrote only about cricket. We played golf together and went to the same parties. You did what you liked as long as you did your job on the field.' Had a prurient tabloid press been active in the days of Denis Compton and Bill Edrich, they might not have played enough Tests to merit a stand at Lord's named after each of them.

In the end, there were more ups than downs in Graveney's professional career, but he had smelled failure. For example, he is philosophical about the assertion that he was not reliable, but it probably cost him his place in MCC's team to tour South Africa in 1956/57: 'That really upset me.' Scores of 258 and 164 against the West Indies in 1957 revived his fortunes, but the controversial Australian tour of 1958/59 was another disappointment. 'I don't think his smiling nature fits in with the seriousness of Test cricket,' wrote Jack Fingleton after the series. The selectors at Lord's seemed to agree, and he didn't play for England for three seasons. It was a bad time. Gloucestershire sacked him as captain in favour of an amateur cricketer and obstructed a move next door to Worcestershire, causing him to miss the 1961 season. An appeal to MCC was turned down. He recalls the episode with distaste. 'I don't forget, I forgive,' he says.

On his Test comeback in 1962 he scored 97, 153 and 114 against Pakistan. But he was dropped again after three more Tests on the 1962/63 Australian tour, under Ted Dexter's captaincy. Alan Ross thought that he had batted with more incisiveness than ever before, but he missed two Tests, injured in Sydney and dropped in Brisbane. 'I don't think Ted Dexter liked me very much. I don't know why. It was just one of those things,' he says. Ross regretted that 'the ultimate question mark still hovers accusingly around him.' He was 35. His admirers – there were many, especially in the West Country – believed that Graveney was being punished for his elegance. The selectors at Lord's were accused of prejudice, and the evidence for that was that Graveney appeared in no Tests during three English summers. In two of them, when he scored freely, Worcestershire twice won the Championship. 'I reckon I was the best player in the country then,' he says.

He finally lost hope of a return to Test cricket in 1966 when Basil D'Oliveira was selected ahead of him for the first Test. 'I said to myself, that's it mate, you'll never play for England again.' But Dexter had gone and

10

Doug Insole became Chairman of Selectors. Insole, who had been one of the people who sat in judgement when Graveney was refused an immediate transfer to Worcestershire, now judged that he had matured sufficiently to play for England again, and brought him back for the second Test against the West Indies at Lord's. Graveney celebrated with a dazzling 96. Centuries in the third and fifth Tests confirmed his own confidence in his ability. Until 1969, he played in 24 more Tests, averaging 49.30 in 38 innings. It was the most famous resurrection in English cricket, and it was used as ammunition by his supporters to damn the judgement of Graveney's critics, most of whom were assumed in the West Country to be skulking in the Pavilion at Lord's.

After he had retired from first-class cricket, Graveney was able to see a pattern in his Test career. He writes in one of the three books he turned out: 'I had two Test careers, pre-1966 and post 1966. The difference from my point of view was that the second time round I was a man with responsibility. Against Sobers' [West Indian team] I saw myself as the number one batsman. Whether I was or not is of no importance – it was the way I felt and the thought drove me along. In the 1950s I was the schoolboy among adults and as a result I played without conviction. In those days playing alongside Hutton, Compton, May and a handful of great or near-great players, I regarded myself as a nonentity and consequently I played like one . . . For years I listened to amateur psychiatrists condemning my temperament as unsuitable for the big occasion. It never seemed to matter how I got out, it was always my temperament that caused it. The whole theory was rubbish, yet until now when I can stand on my record, I was never in a position to say so. The fact of the matter is that the more responsibility I have the better I play. And before 1966 I was not getting my share.'

He actually captained England in the fourth Test against Australia 1968, although he had a hand injury, and he had already turned 40 just before he played his favourite innings at Lord's – 151 in 1967 against India's trio of masterful spin bowlers, Chandrasekhar, Bedi and Prasanna, on an uncovered wicket with the ball taking lumps out of the pitch and turning square. By happy chance, he was batting with Basil D'Oliviera. Graveney is one of the heroes in D'Oliviera's poignant story. Only two years earlier, Graveney had himself convinced D'Oliviera, who was playing Lancashire League cricket, that there was a future for him at Worcestershire. Once the move was made, D'Oliveira scored heavily, and took enough wickets to get into the England team in 1966. In the Test against India, Graveney was 70 not out overnight. The next morning he scored 80 out of the 107 the pair of them put on before lunch. 'It was one of those mornings when everything hit the middle of the bat. Basil said I was making him look like an idiot. He told me to piss off.'

His all-time favourite performance was 118 in three hours against the West Indies in Trinidad in January 1968, the same year he was awarded the OBE, (he thinks he was the only professional cricketer who was honoured while he was still playing). It was the same year that saw the exclusion of D'Oliviera from the original team to tour South Africa that winter. Graveney had helped D'Oliveira to get back in the England team after he had been dropped after the first Test, and a bad tour of the West Indies the previous winter. When one of the batsmen was injured before the Oval Test against Australia, Colin Cowdrey telephoned Graveney: 'I said he was back at what he used to be.' Advice taken, D'Oliveira was reselected, and he seemed to have guaranteed a place on the winter tour with 158 at the Oval. When the news of his rejection arrived at the county ground in Worcester, Graveney's first furious reaction was to say that if Basil was not going, neither was he. Graveney, who had sent D'Oliveira home after he had burst into tears, says: 'I got him into the first-class game. My responsibility was to see he did well, but Colin [Cowdrey, the captain] didn't do him any favours, and neither did Doug Insole. It was an unsavoury episode which grew out of the culture at MCC of that time, and that was dictatorial.'

His wife Jackie was more surprised than Tom by the offer of the Presidency of MCC. She knew him not just as a husband and a professional cricketer, but as a rebel who had regularly been in conflict with the authorities at Lord's. He had sat in the Pavilion in 1969, watching Middlesex against

Lancashire when he should have been playing for Worcestershire, waiting for the result of a hearing into a charge of a serious breach of discipline. This was a complicated business to do with money and poor communication. It was Graveney's benefit year (in which he played friendly games intended to raise money for his retirement) and he was anxious to play in a Sunday League game that was scheduled to take place on the rest day of the Old Trafford Test against the West Indies. When he mentioned this to Alec Bedser, then the Chairman of Selectors, he was told he could not play in the friendly game on the Sunday in the middle of the Test match. 'In that case', he replied, 'don't pick me'.

When he was chosen, Graveney assumed that the selectors had tacitly agreed to let him play on Sunday, though no one had spelled that out. Bedser said he had told Graveney on the Wednesday before the Test that he must not play on Sunday. Graveney swears that not until close of play on the first day, the Thursday, did Bedser remind him of the Sunday prohibition. He played nonetheless, and the game raised more than £1,000 – a signification proportion of his total benefit of £7,000.

When he appeared at Lord's the following Thursday in front of a panel chaired by Edmund King of Warwickshire, Graveney stood no chance. In those days disciplinary panels were not deterred by lawyers or agents. Bedser was told not to pick Graveney for the next three Tests and that was the end of it. He never played for England again. 'It was a miserable way to finish. I wasn't very pleased,' he said, looking wistfully out at the square from a box in the Mound Stand. But his forgiving nature gets the better of him. Now he describes King as 'a lovely man', and says, of Bedser: 'That's over. We don't bear grudges.' If equable did not exist as an adjective, it might have been invented to describe Tom Graveney. But his brushes with authority explain why one senior figure at MCC said, during Graveney's term, 'Tom Graveney has more reason to love Lord's than MCC.'

At the time of that last Test he was 42. When he finally retired from county cricket in 1971, he coached in Queensland for a year. Back home, he became a publican, running the Royal Oak in Prestbury near Cheltenham racecourse for a couple of years. Graveney was up every morning at six to look after the cellar; Jackie Graveney said it was the first proper job he'd had in his life. In the 1980s his West Country burr and his shrewd judgements of cricketers became familiar on BBC radio and TV. He remained in demand for celebrity appearances on occasions such as the Governor of the Bank of England's annual cricket match, and he hosted a box in the Mound Stand which kept him in touch with new generations of MCC committee men, such as Charles Fry. He continued to appear in charity matches. Vic Marks, then of Somerset now of the *Observer*, remembers Graveney snicking the ball through the slips and saying to him, 'Don't get out, we want to watch you bat.' He thought he had played his last game at the age of 67, when he clipped a six off Mark Nicholas's bowling and scored 14 in the last over to win the match. 'I'm retiring after that,' he said. But he was prevailed on to appear for the Lord's Taverners against an MCC President's XI when he was 68. He was caught David Frost, the TV interviewer, bowled Robert Powell, the actor, for 1. That really was the end.

He remains active in organisations that flourish at cricket's grassroots, such as the League Cricket Conference and the Council of Cricket Societies. In his late seventies, he lives in Cheltenham in a comfortable house just down the road from Cheltenham College's cricket field, and he continues to play golf, despite having acquired two new hips and a pacemaker. When he was playing seriously, his grip was the same for golf and cricket. He has never lost it.

Graveney is still outspoken. 'I was struck by the strength of his opinions. He might prove to be an exciting and not entirely diplomatic President,' says Charles Fry. Graveney doubted whether it was morally right to send a team to Zimbabwe in 2004. And he is a persistent critic of the ECB for its neglect of grassroots cricket, and for allowing so much to be spent on overseas players. He would insist that a minimum of eight of a county XI should be qualified for England. He is mildly contemptuous of businessmen who think they know how to run county clubs ('know nothings') and declares that it is absurd, in an Ashes summer, for counties to hire Australians to play before the Tests begin: 'Why should we give them a bit of practice?' At the outset of his Presidency he wondered whether MCC could play a larger role in recreational cricket and was anxious to do something dramatic to arrest the virtual elimination of cricket in state schools: 'In twelve months, I can't do much, but I'll be trying.'

The sweetness and authority of his cover-drive still linger in the collective memory. To the millions who began to watch cricket after he had retired, the name of Graveney has become synonymous with batsmanship inspired by elegance and style, rather than by a single-minded determination to accumulate runs. But that does not entirely explain the affection cricket-lovers feel towards Graveney. It is hard to resist the conclusion that the traits identified by Len Hutton as weaknesses – his open, smiling face, sunny nature and the love of cricket for its own sake – are the strengths that make him a good companion and a shrewd choice as President of MCC.

THE GROUNDSMAN'S LAMENT

The new year at Lord's may have started officially when Tom Graveney took office, but the reality is that it begins the day after the last game of the season. On 12 September Middlesex's Sven Koenig bowled the last over in his last game at Lord's, finishing in a draw against Northamptonshire, and the players trudged back to their dressing rooms in the Lord's Pavilion for the last time that summer. Straight away Mick Hunt, the head groundsman, got down to the serious business of preparing the square for the summer of 2005: 'September is as important as any time in the calendar,' he says, sitting in the cabin at the Nursery End where he and his crew shelter from the elements.

Hunt, who has the weathered face of a countryman, was born in St John's Wood, a stone's throw from Lord's. His father had been a good enough cricketer to play for the Army at the end of the Second World War when he got tonked round the ground by an Australian Air Force pilot named Keith Miller. Mick loved playing cricket and when he discovered he was not good enough to play it for a living, he decided a job on the ground staff was the next best thing. He joined Lord's 36 years ago, and took over as head groundsman in 1984.

The 2004 season had begun earlier than ever before, on 9 April, and the last county game finished sixteen weeks later. There are eighteen pitches on Hunt's square and the best of them had been used in two five-day Tests and four one-day internationals (ODIs). 'There were seven major matches in

2004,' he says. 'Not another ground in the world has that many.' Two or three games had been played on each of the pitches, and Hunt's diagnosis was exhaustion. He believes too much cricket is being played at Lord's. 'Someone's got to say enough is enough.' Not that the members will say enough is enough. Their complaint is that there is too little.

It's not all bad news in Hunt's world, however. 'Pitches are far better nowadays,' he says. 'The technology is improving. Draining machines have more blades and are finer, and equipment like a hydrostatic roller goes so slow that we get maximum contraction. Grass seed is better, and there's more research going into it.' Hunt is the company pitch doctor, who treats the square as if it were an invalid badly in need of rest and repair. But there is a bit of a farmer in him too because he can usually find something to complain about.

In September, each of seventeen pitches gets a dose of ten bags of a cocktail of soil containing carefully balanced proportions of clay – about 30 per cent – and sand. Too much clay and the soil won't dry; too much

Head Groundsman Mick Hunt looks relaxed – only a temporary state.

sand and it won't bind. Spread evenly. This turns the brilliant green square a shade of brown. To combat wear and tear, Hunt then seeds the square with ryegrass ('deeper rooting, less susceptible to disease'). Except on a couple of pitches that had been used late in the season, it took well. By the end of October, the grass had begun to grow. The race was on to get it established before winter started, but the emerald-green look was coming back, especially in the middle of the square where the major matches are played. Now that the outfield is used more regularly for fielding practice ('cricketers play rugby out there now') Hunt nurses it carefully, feeding with fertiliser and root stimulants, inspecting constantly for signs of disease. In an open space like the Nursery Ground next door, the wind helps to blow disease away. In the playing area, hemmed in by high stands, Hunt's crew have to do the job of the wind.

Hunt's second job in September 2004 was to complete a task that had begun in 1991, when the first of the eighteen pitches in the square was dug up and re-laid. Hunt had persuaded MCC's Cricket Committee that the reputation of Lord's was being damaged by pitches that were tired and old, making them low and slow: 'It was like having a fantastic car whose engine wouldn't work. I was embarrassed.' He says the nine-foot slope from the Grand Stand down to the Tavern Stand is irrelevant: it merely exaggerates seam movement. Stands are more influential: 'The ball tends to swing more because the ground is enclosed. Batsmen think it's seaming, but mostly it's swinging.'

Since three or four years go by before a re-laid pitch produces pace and bounce, the decision to re-lay the whole square was a long-term commitment. The last of the pitches, newly-laid in 2004, will not be tested until a one-day league game in 2006, and will not be ready for a four-day game before 2007 – at the earliest. Hunt is glad the job is over, and is pleased with the result. The consensus among players, umpires and the media is that Lord's now has a good cricket wicket. The new pitches, says Hunt, are 'not frighteningly quick' but have 'good carry to the 'keeper'. Keeping it that way requires constant vigilance.

Mick Hunt lives in a square block of three flats overlooking the Nursery Ground, which is a necessity rather than a convenience. Each winter morning he is out on the square, brushing it to keep off the dew. Damp roots encourage disease, and the brushing helps circulate air around the roots. He is particularly attentive to the grass on the middle of the square where the next summer's major matches will take place, and England will play Australia in July. 'It's never out of your mind; you're always preparing those pitches. To me, they're like a magnet,' he says.

Winter is no time for idleness, on or off the ground. Late in 2004, when they get the next season's fixture list, Hunt and John Stephenson, the Head of Cricket, make the pitch plan for the coming season. Each pitch has a number, and there is a system for deciding how they will be distributed through the season. The big-match pitches for Test and important one-day games will be numbers eight to ten. The first game will be on pitch number three, nearest to the Grand Stand, and the second on pitch six, because Hunt always works down the Lord's slope. When a pitch lying high on the slope is watered, moisture seeps down the slope to dampen the pitches further down. You don't need to be a Nobel Prize-winner to work it out, but there is nothing haphazard about deciding which teams will play on which pitches in 2005.

Hunt now subcontracts the most arduous business of a groundsman's winter, which is aerating the earth by spiking it. When it was done manually, the ground staff spent a good slice of winter doing it once and then doing it again. A groundsman's life has been made easier by modern technology. The drive to innovate comes from golf courses, which have even more grass to be cared for. The machine that aerates large areas is called a Vertidrain, a clumsy name which succeeds in describing its function. It is brutish, square, and a little forbidding as it crawls across the outfield aerating it with rows of vicious spikes called tines.

Aeration is badly needed on the Lord's outfield, which was re-laid in the winter of 2002 with specially grown turf on a sandy soil that drains quickly. The idea was to get the players back into the game as soon as possible after

rain. The problem with sandy soil is that it turns very hard. It needs a Vertidrain's power-driven tines to pierce the whole outfield to a depth of eight to ten inches. The contractor's man takes two days to cover the whole outfield in October, again in December and in January. In February, Hunt brings in a Microtine, which, as the name suggests, is smaller and precise enough to be allowed on to the sacred square.

January is for maintenance work on the mowers and rollers that occupy two spacious garages. Engineers check the motor that moves the big and heavy sight screen at the Nursery End. The sight screen makes Hunt nervous. 'My heart misses a beat when the umpire signals for the screen to be moved, because it's a hell of a contraption. You hope the outside contractors do it right.' An automatic brake mechanism prevents it being

LAWNMOWERS IN THE WORKSHOP: *'While Oxford and Cambridge battle it out on the immaculate cricket pitch, the lawnmowers, rollers and other mad machines are taking a well earned break in the cool shade of their workshops (yes it is hot and sunny out there today) before owner and steed are back on centre stage for more synchronized formation mowing, rolling and whatever else the pitch demands! I'm not missing out on the cricket as from here I can see the Ladies' Match on the Nursery Ground'.*

moved by hand, and Hunt's nightmare is that one day this will break down in the middle of a Test. Despite the size of the screen, Mark Ramprakash complained that he lost a ball from a tall fast bowler like Curtly Ambrose in the shade between the sight screen and the NatWest Media Centre. The three white drapes Hunt placed above the screen symbolise Ramprakash's legacy at Lord's.

Making his daily pilgrimage to the middle in January 2005, Hunt liked what he saw. Because the grass had not stopped growing during a mild winter, it was a good, bright green. 'We just nipped it to keep it presentable. We don't want it too long or woolly,' he says. The grass was fed and inspected for disease. In the olden days, which is anything more than 25 years ago, a groundsman would simply apply an all-purpose winter feed. Thanks to golf courses, there is now more variety in the feeds, though it does not come cheap. Partly because of the cost, Hunt sprays the square with insecticides only sparingly.

Cricket cannot be not far off when the roller trundles across the outfield on to the square in March. In Hunt's old-style calendar, rolling started at the same time as the Cheltenham National Hunt Festival, but the match scheduled for pitch three – MCC v. Warwickshire, the Champion county – was to begin on 8 April. This was one day earlier than the same game in 2004, which itself held the record for the first cricket at Lord's, and Hunt's schedule has to be brought forward. He is disgruntled: 'I find it a bit ridiculous, starting this early.'

The light, 36-inch roller – weight about 10 cwt. – started work on the surface of the square before the end of February. The weight is increased by putting more water into the rollers as ballast, from 15 cwt., to 30 and finally 50 cwt. When the square is ready, the rollers will have followed their slow rhythm backwards and forwards across the square for 80 hours, spending between four and five hours on each wicket. Because of the unpredictability of the weather, Hunt starts the process early. As soon as it rains, work stops. The weather turned nasty late in February but the work was finished in time for 8 April.

Hunt wore a woollen hat to keep out the wind and rain which stopped play on the first day of the season. The first pitch of the season was bland, a good wicket for Nick Knight, who got the first hundred of the season on 9 April, and Alastair Cook, the 20-year-old Essex opening bat, who scored a hundred in MCC's first innings and fell only 3 runs short of a second as MCC won by seven wickets. Despite the weather and Hunt's instinctive pessimism, the square and the outfield looked great.

LORD'S: A CONDUCTED TOUR

In 1949, when Tom Graveney played his first game on the ground, Lord's was a very different place. After the Second World War, Lord's stood on the edge of a no-man's land of electricity sub-stations and car showrooms on the north side of the Regent's Canal. There was a synagogue just across St John's Wood Road, but the fashionable fine detached houses, distinguished Victorian terraces and blocks of flats were to be found north of the ground on the way to the pedestrian crossing in Abbey Road made famous by the Beatles. Not until the 1960s did property developers realise that Lord's might lend some distinction to the neighbourhood. All evidence of industry was eradicated, and an hotel and new blocks of expensive flats sprang up alongside the ground (a distant view of the wicket was said to be a selling point for these flats, but it is very rare to see anyone watching from a balcony). MCC got involved in the property business too. The twelve-storey block which imposes itself on the skyline behind the Pavilion was built on MCC land leased to a developer in 1966 to raise £150,000 when the club was particularly hard up.

The main entrance to Lord's is through the Grace Gates. They were moved thirteen feet down the road when Lord's Tavern was redeveloped, but Graveney would have found the Portland stone columns and the decorated ironwork reassuringly familiar when he returned as President. Built in 1922, to the memory of W. G. Grace, 'The Great Cricketer', the gates celebrate the club as well as the player. The initials MCC, nicely gilded, are part of the ironwork, just under red cricket balls illuminated by the yellow rays of the sun. Three stumps are sculpted into stonework; the side columns are topped by decorated stone urns. Not many of the members who pause to show their passes to the gateman stop to glance back at the gates. A pity; they are worth a second look.

In 1949 the buildings behind the high brick wall were ageing and uncomfortable. The Pavilion was flanked on the left by a small stand, which was low enough to allow spectators to stand behind it, watching and gossiping at the same time. This stand is the scene for a painting that hangs in the Writing Room in the Pavilion – it shows Edward VII, when Prince of Wales, and his wife strolling along the boundary, while his mistress Lillie Langtry sits in the crowded stand (and, incidentally, a fielder makes a good stop on the boundary). A plain concrete stand to the right of the Pavilion separated it from an ivy-covered clock tower where members would take luncheon.

The Grand Stand dominated the northern side of the ground, with Father Time removing a bail from the stumps on the weather vane on the tiled roof above the scoreboard. The stand was designed by Sir Herbert Baker, the distinguished architect of New Delhi and Pretoria, who failed to reproduce the form he showed abroad at home in London. He did not notice, for example, that many of the seats at the sides and the back of the stand had a restricted view of the cricket. At the end of the ground were the open, unreserved seats euphemistically known as the free seats. They weren't actually free, as spectators had already paid to get into the ground.

Crowds at Middlesex games were larger and more vocal when Graveney was playing either for Gloucestershire or Worcestershire. When barracking began, it came from the free seats, or from the pavement in front of the Tavern. Members could never decide whether it was good fun or bad manners. The Tavern was separated from the free seats by the ageing bulk of the Mound Stand, built in 1898 by Frank, son of Thomas Verity who designed the Pavilion. It was a relic of an era in which the comfort of crowds was not a preoccupation. Apart from the Pavilion, there was little of architectural merit at Lord's in 1949.

Because MCC still ran the game, nationally and internationally, Lord's was the headquarters of cricket, all cricket, everywhere. Like the British Empire, MCC relinquished power voluntarily, in the knowledge that if it did not, it would still be lost, but without consultation. But the newly formed International Cricket Council (the ICC) moved into an undistinguished red-brick building next to the ground staff. The England and Wales Cricket Board (the ECB) made its headquarters in a plain modern building hidden away next to the Indoor School at the Nursery End. Perhaps they wanted to distance themselves from their parent, because MCC became a symbol of division and disharmony in English cricket – most clearly when the Cape Coloured England player Basil D'Oliveira was not chosen to tour South Africa in 1968. Attitudes formed by old age and snobbery might not have reflected the views of most members but they seemed to belong to the people who ran the place. Vigorous and vocal critics – and for a time they included Tom Graveney, no less – poured scorn on MCC. Michael Parkinson, by occupation columnist, TV interviewer, and Yorshireman, called MCC the Marylebone Clodpoles Club. But times changed. In 2005, MCC's link to its Imperial past was severed completely when the ICC moved to new headquarters in Dubai, which had not previously been recognised as a cricket centre, but which did offer a benevolent tax regime.

In 1949, when crowds were allowed to spill over on to the grass, Lord's held more spectators than it does today. When it is full now, it holds 29,500 spectators, give or take a few hundred – a paltry number compared to the 100,000 at the Melbourne Cricket Ground or Eden Gardens in Kolkata. Sydney's and Mumbai's Test grounds each hold twice as many as Lord's. But it is neither authority nor size that attracts the visitors who turn up each day to take a conducted tour of Lord's, and over the year number 30,000 (at £8 a time for adults, a nice little earner). They are there because of the great players and the memorable matches of the past, and for the sight of the New Lord's. Instead of the forbidding title of 'Headquarters of Cricket', it now describes itself more amiably as the 'Home of Cricket'. The mystery has diminished, but the magic remains – otherwise why would the great Indian

batsman Rahul Dravid bring his family to Lord's, paying at the kiosk to take them on the tour and show them where he made 95 for India on his first tour of England in 1996?

I join a tour on a chilly, damp day in spring. There are fifteen of us, a little melting pot from cricket-playing nations – India, Australia, New Zealand and South Africa, plus an unlikely group of young American girls. Our guide is an MCC member called Colin Tonge, and he manages to pull off the clever trick of not patronising those who know little or nothing about cricket while satisfying the curiosity of those who do.

We start at the Grace Gates, a memorial, he explains, to 'the greatest player in the history of the game'. No Australian contests this assertion, which reflects an instinctive feeling that the history of cricket somehow

... the horrible events of Thursday have not deterred the diverse crowds pouring through the Grace Gates; and the usually tight security is ... Just that little bit tighter and anything unusual is given a thorough going over ...

THE GRACE GATES: '*Sunday 10th July 2005 – It's the Natwest One-Day Challenge between England and Australia – the horrible events of Thursday have not deterred the diverse crowds pouring through the Grace Gates, and the usually tight security is just that little bit tighter and anything unusual is given a thorough going over – such as my compact fold-out paint box, which I guess not too many others will be carrying! A two-minute silence is observed to remember all of those affected three days ago… and then life and cricket carries on.*'

belongs at Lord's. As we move towards the Pavilion, we pass the Allen Stand, which, Tonge explains, is named after an amateur cricketer named Allen, 'Gubby' Allen, who in 1932/33 refused to bowl Bodyline, a vicious form of fast bowling designed by Douglas Jardine, the captain of England, to combat Don Bradman, who was actually the greatest player in the history of the game. But the stand was not named after Allen because he was an English Test cricketer. Allen was an MCC member for 51 years, and for many of them he ran MCC in much the same way as he behaved in Australia: stubbornly and as he thought best.

The Harris Garden, which sits behind the Allen Stand, is another memorial to a player who became an influential administrator at Lord's. We learn that Lord Harris was also Governor of Bombay in the 1890s, which causes the Indians in the party to exchange glances. Harris gets mixed reviews for his role in Indian cricket. Schools in Mumbai still play for the Harris Trophy. But he did not play with Indians, and his love of cricket did not make them dislike him any less. The nicest thing we learn about Harris, who died aged 81, having had his way at MCC for decades, is that his enthusiasm for the game never waned.

On past the Middlesex office which runs county cricket, which has been played at Lord's since 1876. We pause at the entrance at the back of the Pavilion where Tonge explains that doormen make sure that members and their guests are properly dressed (people on the tour can wear what they please). He asks us to estimate MCC's annual subscription fee: an Australian says $10,000 Australian; an American suggests US$5,600. Tonge lets them know that the price of privilege is not so inflated in London. MCC membership costs the equivalent of A$825 or US$600.

We are ushered into the Long Room where the gas fires are on, the chairs are laid out facing the ground and the walls are hung with old paintings. It feels like a large, comfortable drawing room in a big house that doubles as a sports ground. Seen through the capacious windows, the playing area is a luscious emerald-green. We are asked to look at a portrait of W. G. Grace, if for no other reason than that he is wearing brown boots. No one knows why. We go on to a painting of a cricket match in 1740, which Tonge uses as a pretext to point out that MCC, founded in 1787, is a year older than Australia, and, incidentally, that the Thomas Lord who founded Lord's and moved it to the present site in 1814, was, unlike Harris, not a Lord himself. In the bar behind the Long Room great players like Keith Miller and Denis Compton compete for attention with a black and white photograph of a very great athlete indeed, perhaps, as he always said himself, the greatest. Muhammad Ali is seen sitting, somewhat incongruously, on the players' balcony drinking a cup of tea. Outside, we clamber over the seats on the first balcony. Peering into the visitors' dressing room, one of the women on the tour observes that there are no curtains. Obvious questions are left unspoken.

In the real tennis court behind the Pavilion we are treated to a brief history of a game that dates from medieval Europe, when it became the game of kings and courtiers. Tonge intrigues the Americans when he explains that the 'server' and the 'service' in modern lawn tennis are relics of that ancient time when a prince preferred to have one of his servants put the ball in play. In the Museum next door the prize exhibit is the tiny urn that contains the Ashes. English cricket had been pronounced dead in 1882 after a brilliant Australian win in the Oval Test, and the ashes of what is believed to be a burned bail were later placed in this receptacle in mock commemoration. Tonge explains that the small terracotta urn was so fragile that MCC declared it simply could not be moved, even when Australia won these Ashes in series after series. But the urn has now been restored, and a journey is no longer out of the question.

The tour continues round the perimeter of the ground, past the Warner Stand, an undistinguished affair named after Sir Pelham Warner, who managed the tour during which 'Gubby' Allen refused to bowl Bodyline. With the exception of the Compton (Denis) and Edrich (Bill) Stands at the end of the ground, the buildings are now monuments not to old administrators or players but to outstanding architects. Sir Nicholas Grimshaw designed the Grand Stand that replaced Sir Herbert Baker's. A high central mast supports hangers from which the roof is suspended. Seats in the front rows of the stand are close to the boundary edge, and the side-on views of the wicket are splendid. Anyone who says it is a shame not to be able to see the movement of the ball from behind the bowler's arm should know that Sir Don Bradman would have recommended watching the batsman's feet. The Grand Stand was finished in 1997, and it is properly named: it is very grand indeed.

The Media Centre, which sits slightly uncomfortably between the Compton and Edrich stands, is one of the most famous modern buildings in London, maybe in the nation. By selecting a unique design by a firm called Future Systems that had never been tested in practice, MCC took a remarkable risk and was rewarded with no fewer than seven architectural awards. There was a sense of anticipation as Tonge's party entered the lifts at the bottom of the two pylons that support the smooth lines of the aluminium pod. We learned that it is constructed of 32 aluminium sections. A huge concave window at the front overlooks play and a smaller window at the rear has a view of the Nursery Ground – which we are told is three and a half acres in extent, and is so called because it is on the site of a nursery garden that grew flowers and vegetables. The Nursery End, where players

*Hacks at work. Journalists have a lofty view
in the NatWest Media Centre.*

practice in the nets during the season, becomes a cricket ground in September. It is overlooked by the Indoor School – another award-winning building. The Nursery Pavilion, without ever finding it, seeks inspiration from the Mound Stand; it is used to feed sponsors and their corporate guests, and for conferences, trade fairs and lectures.

The interior of the Media Centre is coloured a maritime blue, and has four rows of long desks. The tour party is struck by the great panoramic view of the ground from the press box, and the comfortable area for food and drink. It is not in Tonge's brief, nor is it my position at the time, to point out that the people who respond with least enthusiasm to the Media Centre are the people it houses – the media. MCC's management is irritated by criticism of their celebrated building, but commentators and journalists do not like the sealed-in space, and object to the air-conditioning outlets cluttering the desks on which they write. Only the BBC, which insisted on an opening window as a condition of moving from its comfortable berth in the Pavilion, gets any fresh air.

Finally Tonge asks us to inspect the Mound Stand, the most exotic of the new buildings, opened in 1987. It was built at a time when MCC could ill afford it – until Sir Paul Getty, a prince of philanthropists, bailed them out by donating half the total cost of £4.35m. Designed by Michael Hopkins and Partners, it is a brilliant fusion of old and new, conservation and modernism. Hopkins retained the existing terrace and its graceful supporting brick walls, and floated down on it another tier of seats covered by a fantastical roof of tented membranes, made of PVC. The theory was that the tent-like shapes should symbolise cricket as a festival. The top of a lift shaft at the side of the Mound Stand is the new home for Father Time.

Facing us, on our way out of the Mound Stand, are a pair of forbidding iron gates which look as though they were built to repel all borders. In fact they celebrate the bicentenary of MCC in 1987 and were given by the Duke of Westminster in memory of Viscount Cobham, his grandfather and another of MCC's grandees. On the way back to the Grace Gates, Tonge pointed out the original site of Lord's Tavern, which symbolised something else about cricket – the indelible link between watching it and drinking, though Tonge did not put it like that. Before we leave, we are invited to visit the shop at the East Gate, which sells replica and other casual clothing, and souvenirs of Lord's, and is a nice big earner for MCC.

On our tour, Colin Tonge also thinks it worth mentioning the current President of MCC. 'He's an old 'un now, but he was a great cricketer, called Tom Graveney. He was a professional cricketer and it's the first time in all these years that a professional has been President of MCC. He's unique.' This walk-on part in the Lord's tour suggests that, 56 years since he first trod on its turf, Graveney is part of the fabric and the history of the place.

A CAROL SERVICE

The week before Christmas Tom Graveney had his pacemaker checked before flying to South Africa to watch the Christmas and New Year Tests. ('It's still working'). BBC TV had interviewed him after England's win in the first Test in Port Elizabeth, their eighth in succession. He spoke of his excitement at the performance of Andrew Strauss, who scored 126 and 94 not out: he detected a touch of John Edrich in him. After nearly three months as President he was adjusting to his new role: 'I've enjoyed most of it. It's a total change for me, suddenly coming in from the fringe right into the middle of the game.' It had certainly been a while since the BBC were so keen to interview him for his opinions on English cricket.

He had been chauffeured to London from Cheltenham to attend committee meetings a couple of times a week on average, and sometime three. He confessed that, without the car and driver, he could not do the job. He had enjoyed getting to know the staff, and marvelled at the efficiency of Stephanie Lawrence, Roger Knight's personal assistant, who was in charge of his diary. Before he left for South Africa, he had one more Presidential duty to perform, on 16 December, at MCC's annual carol service. Since the Pavilion was out of bounds, the Museum had been specially decorated, and Graveney decided to make it a family outing, with Jackie, their son and his wife and daughter. But they were not joined by the usual crowd of loyal members, whose presence could be relied on to raise the average age of any MCC audience. The service is an exercise in trying to get the neighbours in

33

THE CHRISTMAS CAROL CONCERT: '*Thursday 16th December 2004 – It's Christmas Carol Concert time in the cricket museum. With the aroma of Christmas trees and mulled wine, essential ingredients, as well as the mince pies wafting past me, the atmosphere is set. The crowds arrive, the choir enters and rousing rounds of carols are sung, interspersed liberally with breaks to refill mulled wine glasses and plates with mince pies, to result in a festive evening all in a very good cause.*'

St John's Wood on side. The audience is local and the collection goes to St John's Hospice in Grove End Road, round the corner from Lord's.

This is not just good community relations; it is also shrewd local politics. There are a number of things the neighbours do not like – the crowds, the noise, and the prospect of floodlights. After MCC was refused permission to stage the first Twenty20 cup final in 2003 because of local objections, a group

called 'Local to Lord's' was established so that dialogue might take place. It has had some success. The following year Middlesex was allowed to play Surrey in a Twenty20 game before the largest crowd to watch a county game at Lord's in more than 50 years. The lights were only a potential problem. Test grounds now need lights, not to play at night, but to improve natural light during the day. But the greater problem was to find a form of flood-lighting that would illuminate the playing area without spoiling the elegance of the sightlines on the ground. Graveney judged that irritation was caused, not by lights or even music, but by the crowds. An invasion of around 27,500 men, women and children in an expensive residential area inevitably disrupts local life.

Consequently, the VIPs at the carol service were the Deputy Mayor of

Westminster, and his wife, and local people were much in evidence in the congregation. Bright lights, harmonious music from the London Chorus, and an agreeable crush: 'Marvellous,' said Graveney, but what he liked best of all was his granddaughter at the end of the evening, when she approached Roger Knight, a tall man, craned her neck, and said: 'Thank you for a very nice evening, Roger. Have a Happy Christmas.' Graveney glows: 'She's only five.'

ON THE CRICKET COMMITTEE

Tony Lewis, the only Welshman to captain England, is a past President of MCC. He wrote the official history of MCC for its 200th anniversary in 1987, and now he is an amiable and tough-minded chairman of the committee that ought to define what MCC is about, the Cricket Committee. MCC spends £1.3m a year on what is loosely called the recreational game. Club members make up MCC teams that play 450 games against schools and clubs each summer, and touring teams visit nations as diverse, and unlikely, as Estonia and Japan. One grey day in the depth of winter, I sat in on the Cricket Committee. Tony Lewis opened the meeting by welcoming Tom Graveney. 'It's always good to have the President here,' he said. Graveney, wearing a red cardigan under his blue blazer, looked cheerful and rosy-cheeked.

A long agenda took members through a draft of a five-year-plan, university cricket, and the playing membership, including the new women's division. Darrell Hair, the Australian Test umpire who now works for MCC as a specialist on the Laws of Cricket, reported on the latest controversy about bowlers suspected of throwing. In the last light of the day, papers were being shuffled into neat piles by committee men who wanted to make a quick getaway when Graveney pointed out that they had not looked over the page at the last item on the agenda. This was youth cricket and particularly getting cricket back into state schools that have opted out, an issue that is close to Graveney's heart.

THE NEW ROOF TERRACE: '*Wednesday 25th April and Friday 13th May 2005 – Well, rain stopped play due to a rather forceful thunderstorm, when I first started to sketch, but on the Friday afternoon on the third day of the Middlesex and Gloucestershire contest the sun came out and the new roof terrace is a veritable sun trap with glazing to protect against the winds and the unsightly roof plant now hidden behind frosted screens and wood panels behind the spectators.*'

There was buzz about a new campaign to bring cricket back to state schools. Mark Nicholas, Channel 4 commentator, had enlisted the support of distinguished figures such as Mervyn King, the Governor of the Bank of England, a dedicated Worcestershire supporter. Big guns like King would be required if the fundraising target of £25m was to be met. Nicholas had already tested the water at Lord's, but the reaction was that he had been

m, when I first started to sketch, but on the Friday afternoon on the third day of the Middlesex and Gloucestershire contest – the sun came out and the new roof terrace is a desirable scene to be flying to perform against the birds

Karen Neale

vague about details MCC thought were important. Getting kids who are deprived of the opportunity to play cricket is like motherhood – no one is against it. But it turned out that reactions on the Cricket Committee were neither unanimous, nor straightforward.

Some members argued fiercely that cricket was not capable of being revived in state schools. Give them money for new facilities, and pavilions would be torched, equipment nicked and pitches dug up. Not everyone was so pessimistic. Nicholas had wanted to know whether MCC would support the appeal or not. Some felt strongly that he was making a claim on money that ought to be spent by MCC on its own programme. Others were anxious to know how their money would be spent, and whether it would be properly audited. The odd voice said MCC should continue to talk to the organisers.

The question was finally defined: was it better to encourage children by spending money in schools, or by urging cricket clubs to organise youth teams and coaching sessions? Had a vote been taken, it would have gone heavily in favour of the clubs. 'Fair enough,' said Graveney. 'It's not cricket for schools but for schoolchildren. We want children of school age playing cricket.'

The Cricket Committee is the apex of MCC's sprawling amateur cricket programme. John Stephenson, the former county cricketer who became Head of Cricket in the summer of 2004, inherited a cricket programme that was already generously financed, and shortly after his arrival it grew even larger. MCC had always encouraged youth cricket by playing against schools and employing talented young cricketers at Lord's. Until 1965, these young men were part of the Ground Staff and they were expected to bowl to members in the nets – the member was expected to tip five shillings by leaving two half crowns on the top of a stump. The most distinguished of them were Denis Compton and Ian Botham, who, like the others, did manual work with the groundsmen, and sold scorecards on match days.

Now it is Cricket Staff rather than Ground Staff, and when they are not playing cricket, they are getting their first lessons in coaching and grounds-manship. A group of seventeen young men between eighteen and twenty-two and two women play competitively throughout the summer, and they come to Lord's with the same objective – they want to play professional cricket, though only one in four or five will do so. This is a cricket education.

Stephenson's portfolio starts with the ground itself, and with the Indoor School and its classes for hundreds of children who arrive for coaching in school holidays. Then there is the complex business of organising all those MCC out-matches in the cricket office. His role has now greatly expanded following MCC's decision to move into University Cricket. It is a proper job.

John Stephenson was an accomplished all-rounder in county cricket for Essex and Hampshire: in nineteen seasons he had scored 14,772 runs at 32.53 and taken 397 wickets at 32.6, and was one of England one-cap wonders, playing in the Oval Test against Australia in 1989. He was 39 at the start of the 2004 season and contemplating retirement. Early in the spring, he happened to fall in with an Army officer who told him that he was resigning his commission so that he could apply to be MCC's Head of Cricket. Stephenson says: 'This was the job I'd always wanted. I didn't know whether I'd get it but I went hell for leather after it.' The deadline for applications was only a week away. He went straight on the short-list and was recalled for a second interview.

Early in the season, he was in and out of the Essex team, though he had a good game at Durham, where he scored 40 and took 5 for 75 in two innings. On the bus that took the Essex team from Chester-le-Street to Cardiff for a game against Glamorgan, he and Nasser Hussain talked about their future. They are as different as chalk and cheese, but as cricketers they were like twins. They played schools cricket against each other, both attended Durham University and were colleagues as young men at Essex.

Both were contemplating retirement. Hussain said he might become a teacher so that he could spend more time at home. His hundred against Glamorgan came in his last game of county cricket, though he did not know it. Stephenson, who was left out at Cardiff, had also played his last county game, and he did not know it either. Next stop was Somerset at Taunton. Roger Knight found him there and said they would like to appoint him Head of Cricket. Stephenson resigned from Essex on the spot, and got off to a good start with MCC, scoring 58 against the West Indies tourists, which almost won the game. Hussain's last innings was played in the New Zealand Test at Lord's on the same day Stephenson resigned, a not out hundred. After this he retired from all cricket, but instead of teaching, he joined Sky TV's commentary box, where he was much better paid. Hussain's decision got rather more column inches. The future had come earlier than either of them expected.

Stephenson was delighted: 'I've seen so many of my fellow professionals finish, wondering where they're going next.' For a retiring cricketer, the job at Lord's was a change of pace, requiring as much management skill as judgement of cricketers.

The big expansion of Stephenson's role came with MCC's decision to take over from the ECB responsibility for the six university centres of excellence. In olden days Oxford and Cambridge spawned generations of brilliant batsmen who also captained England. Think of the list – Peter May, Colin Cowdrey, Ted Dexter, all of whom became Presidents of MCC, and Mike Brearley, who was not interested. Nor was Mike Atherton, but he was last of a line that appears to have dried up completely. The dominance of Oxbridge declined sharply as a new breed of admissions tutors showed little sympathy for promising cricketers like Cowdrey, ostensibly a student of geography, but not to the extent of writing his final exams.

John Stephenson, MCC Head of Cricket at his 'garden' gate.

The ECB had reorganised six universities into University Centres of Cricketing Excellence (UCCEs). This meant that Oxford University was amalgamated with a former polytechnic called Oxford Brookes as Oxford UCCE. After Cambridge formed an alliance with Anglia Polytechnic, both the ancient universities were able to select students who would not have got into Oxford or Cambridge. The impact was dramatic. By 2004, only one Oxford University undergraduate played for Oxford UCCE, and no more than a couple for Cambridge. For the game at Lord's between Oxford and Cambridge, now reduced to a one-day affair, only bona fide Oxbridge students were eligible to play. Lewis Carroll, who wrote *Alice in Wonderland* in Oxford, would have understood.

For years, Oxford and Cambrige had clung on to first-class status, which meant that their batting and bowling averages appeared in the same tables as those of Test and county cricketers. This flew in the face of clear evidence that both Loughborough and Durham Universities produced better cricketers, yet neither had first-class status. The ECB solution was to extend it, first to Durham and then to Loughborough, but not to the other two UCCEs, Cardiff and Leeds/Bradford, presumably because they were not excellent enough.

By the turn of the century, the England and Wales Cricket Board was finding university cricket a chore. They grudged the £300,000 a year spent on the six UCCEs and were delighted when MCC showed an interest in taking over. Ted Dexter, President in 2001/02, encouraged MCC to spend more of its income directly on cricket, and Tony Lewis and a majority of the Cricket Committee thought the universities were worth MCC money. (A minority thought MCC had other things to spend it on.) Shortly after Stephenson's arrival, MCC agreed, not just to take over, but to increase the annual subsidy to each team from £50,000 to £65,000. MCC guaranteed £1.2 million over three years. In return, the UCCEs were to be known as MCC Universities; players and coaches would wear the red and yellow MCC monogram. 'It's going to spearhead MCC cricket for the next five years,' says Lewis.

Stephenson wanted MCC to be hands-on angels: 'Funding's the easy part, but I don't want to sit back and say 'Here's the money. Get on with it.' MCC members were deputed to be mentors and monitors, to help each of the teams with financial management and coaching. Early recruits to this group were Robin Marlar (Cambridge, Sussex and the *Sunday Times*) and Mike Turner (who was secretary of Leicestershire during some good years). Stephenson argued that the first year would be trial and error, but he never doubted the concept: 'It fits nicely into our development programme. It sits nicely with MCC.'

Stephenson is a well-organised person, lean, neatly turned out, unostentatiously well-mannered. He describes his own personality by contrasting it with Hussain's: 'I'm a stickler for doing what you're told. At Essex, we were told we couldn't wear jeans on an away trip. He used blatantly to break the rules, which was disrespectful. More than that, it was taking my mind off my cricket. I had to say something.' No doubt he did. And he could still play. He is one of the few people at Lord's who still asks for a net, and in the first game of the season, he returned to first-class cricket as captain of MCC against Warwickshire, the Champion County. He did not get a bat, and conceded 74 runs off 14 overs, but, what the hell, MCC won by seven wickets.

The people who report to Stephenson are indispensable backroom figures at Lord's – Mick Hunt the groundsman, Clive Radley, the head coach at the Indoor School and of MCC's Young Cricketers (YCs), and Rachel Lee, the secretary of the Laws working party. Another who reports to Stephenson is a lean, pleasant and enthusiastic young man called Fraser Stewart, who runs the cricket office. This is where Stewart and two assistants organise the programme of 450 MCC out-matches each summer, plus, in 2005, seven overseas tours. Stewart's predecessor left a month after Stephenson's arrival, and Stewart's office was removed from the Pavilion a couple of weeks after his arrival at Lord's. Moving in with other departments in temporary accommodation in the Tavern and Mound Stands turned out to be a useful learning experience. 'I was amazed to find there were so many people employed here,' he says. For a man whose job is to bring order out of chaos, it was a difficult debut, but Stewart's training helped. He has a law degree and had run a legal support service, but he was working from home, and, when the job came up, decided he was ready for a change. He was also a regular performer at MCC out-matches.

Spectators at a Lord's Test don't think of MCC as a cricket club, but its out-matches are a link with people who play cricket rather than watch it. There are 1,800 playing members of MCC – ten per cent of the membership – and 1,500 of them are active. A few are hyperactive – one member played in 35 games in 2003.

On short winter days, the cricket office arranges the fixture list for the coming season, starting with a two-day game against Wisbech CC in the middle of April, when the east wind still blows in from the Urals. The core of the list comprises games against schools and universities and, to make

MCC on tour: the fixture is in Estonia. The umpire has called a temporary halt to proceedings to allow the pony to trot behind the bowler's arm.

Stewart's life easier, these are normally played on the same day each year. The office always tries to accommodate clubs that ask for a special fixture to celebrate an anniversary. Stewart himself usually takes a team to play at his old school, King's School, at Bruton in Somerset.

Match managers are the links between Stewart and the playing members. There are a hundred of them, and since most fixtures are over-subscribed, they double as selectors. In high summer, on most days in midweek, three or four teams are playing across England, though teams also visit Scotland, Ireland and Wales. Stewart's match managers rarely have difficulty in finding eleven players. Apart from some umpires, no one receives expenses, just the prospect of a decent lunch. 'People like the idea of playing for MCC, and they'll take a day off work to do it,' says Stewart.

Last winter match managers and players still communicated by post and via a primitive website. Stewart and his colleagues were not resisting the latest information technology. Quite the reverse, they were anxious to put the whole system on-line, and soon. But it was taking time. Stewart was still waiting at the start of the season.

About a hundred or so club cricketers are elected to membership each year, after a couple of probationary years, thus avoiding the longeurs of the general waiting list. But Stewart is quick to deny that playing out-matches is a back door to full MCC membership. In place of patience, playing members are required to show commitment. Having been nominated as a candidate and endorsed by someone familiar with their cricket, they must agree to play ten games over two years. A third of them will be discarded, and those who are elected also agree to play fifteen games in the next five years.

Many of the out-matches are at public schools. In five days at the end of April and before the beginning of exams, MCC played Cheltenham, Eton, Repton, Radley, and Uppingham. Stewart took a team to Marlborough 'Yes, we do play established schools we've played for years. They're usually quite strong,' says Stewart. Conscious of the Club's reputation for public-school bias, though, the cricket office encourages requests for games from grammar and comprehensive schools, though they don't get many. There is a sprinkling of grammars, including Tom Graveney's old school Bristol Grammar, but only one comprehensive. Wickersley in Rotherham is on the list, along with the Hackney Community Cricket College. When state schools no longer have grounds of their own, they play at a local club, and if the state-school teams are not strong enough, MCC encourages two or three local schools to make up a team. 'We have problems if a fixture is not strong, but we do try to stick with them,' says Stewart.

The composition of touring sides depends on the destination. Serious tours are known as A tours, and, as the quality of cricket falls, they become B or C tours. In 2005 Namibia and Canada, both World Cup Finalists in 2003, were A tours. France and Estonia were definitely C tours – planned in consultation with the ICC's development department. Playing members are expected to pay their way. For games against teams such as Canada, MCC contained a sprinkling of former professionals such as the former England and Worcestershire left-arm spin bowler Richard Illingworth and Tony Penberthy, a Northamptonshire stalwart. The tour to Japan was captained by Tim O'Gorman, a member of the committee who spent a decade with Derbyshire.

Sounds like fun, except it is not supposed to be all fun. 'It's not just a holiday with some cricket. There's a preaching part to it too,' says Stewart. Each team takes a bounty of £3,000 to spread the gospel by purchasing new equipment. Players are expected to coach at schools and clubs, and if there is an umpire in the party, he teaches too. MCC's reputation regularly precedes the team: 'Often you get red carpet treatment,' says Stewart.

Kate Matheve, the cricket office women's cricket administrator, is not finding life easy. Women's cricket started from scratch when membership was opened to women in 1998, at the second time of asking. Seven years later, there were just enough playing members for nineteen out-matches against opponents ranging in strength from Hereford Cathedral School to Australia. That was four more than in 2004, but, with only 50 or so active playing members, Matheve finds it hard to lengthen the fixture list.

The Indoor School lies beyond the boundary of the Nursery Ground, a handsome, prize-wining building whose quality cannot be fully appreciated by anyone looking at it from the outside. Until the 1990s, cricket schools had been windowless, unlovely buildings, and the original indoor school at Lord's had been no exception. But the architectural prestige that reverberated from Michael Hopkins and Partners' Mound Stand had raised expectations. A competition for the new Indoor School produced a design that shunted Hopkins into second place.

The special attribute of the new Lord's school, opened in 1995, is that the roof admits natural light. Victorian factory buildings took the need for natural light for granted, but not indoor schools. Some Cricket Committee members were so accustomed to the use of artificial lighting in indoor nets that they feared a combination of natural light during the day and artificial light at night would prove unsafe. Mike Gatting was asked to act as guinea pig, and, after a trial, declared himself quite unafraid. Besides the natural light from the roof, the side walls were made to be thrown open on summer afternoons. The building was an immediate success. Now, ten years on, it was due for extensive refurbishment to put in state-of-the-art artificial pitches, each catering for a different style of bowling.

Even on midwinter mornings the school is bathed in quite enough grey light to allow business to proceed. During the summer, Clive Radley, a former Middlesex stalwart, concentrates on MCC Young Cricketers, but at the start of October the focus switches to the indoor school and to the schoolchildren who are encouraged to practise in the nets and to play in six-a-side tournaments. On Fridays the school comes free to London schools: Radley says he enjoys the buzz on days like this. The clients are not always children, however. In December 2004, 29 aspiring coaches from nineteen European countries spent a week learning how to become better coaches.

Radley was a seasoned old pro who retired in 1988 after scoring 26,441 runs in first-class cricket, including two hundreds in only ten Test innings.

His apprenticeship as a coach was with Middlesex 2nd XI, and when Mike Gatting got the job Radley had cherished as 1st XI coach, he moved across to MCC. Those were primitive days, before the widespread use of video recording which allows players to see their faults for themselves and correct them promptly. Video is, Radley declares unequivocally, the greatest single asset of a modern coach.

Parts of the winter are spent judging the candidates for MCC's School of Merit, who are then invited to coaching sessions at the school, and selecting some of the eighteen or so MCC Cricket Staff. In 2004 MCC had managed to lever its team of youngsters into the county championship's 2nd XI competition for the 2005 season. 'That'll stretch us a bit,' says Radley, but that was the idea. Most of the squad come from Britain, but students from Europe, South Africa and Australasia are also eligible for places. One candidate in 2004 lived in Durban, though both parents are English. He completed his matriculation exams on a Friday afternoon, caught the overnight flight to London, and was only a little late for his trial on Saturday morning. His commitment was rewarded with a place. The most accomplished recent graduate is a New Zealander named Hamish Marshall, who made his Test debut in 2000 only two years after graduating from MCC's own academy, and distinguished himself in April 2005 by scoring 160 against Sri Lanka.

School holidays are among the busiest times for Radley's coaching team. Just before Christmas 2004, I watched 20 little boys, each impeccably turned out in white shorts and sweaters, gathered for a session which begins, traditionally, with their being told to take their hands out of their pockets. But it continues in the modern manner: instead of batting or bowling, the drills are for fitness and fielding, starting with press-ups, stretches and a brisk run around the school perimeter. That done, the coaches rolled soft balls towards the boys to pick up and flick in underarm back to the coach.

One of the coaches is tall, balding, and moves with an easy elegance. I would not have recognised him, except that Clive Radley had tipped me off. The children are being taught fielding by the greatest fieldsman since the Second World War, better even than Jonty Rhodes. He had asked whether there was any casual work at Lord's when he came to live in London. His name is Colin Bland, a Rhodesian who played for South Africa from 1961 to 1966. The agility of his pick-up and the speed and accuracy of his return to the stumps was a wonder of the world of cricket. Although the boys were much too young to know who he was, they were in the shadow of a legend. But their grandfathers would have been impressed.

BRANDING THE NEW LORD'S

When David Batts, MCC's deputy chief executive, arrived at Lord's in 2000, he might as well have come from another planet. For a start, he was a businessman. Second, he referred to Lord's as 'the Augusta of cricket'. Batts is a golfer rather than a cricketer, so the comparison with the course that puts on the Masters' Tournament each spring was, from him, high praise: 'Augusta is the pinnacle of experience for a golf tournament,' he says. His point was that Lord's should occupy the same position in international cricket.

Batts spoke the language of modern management, one that had not often been heard at Lord's. His appointment followed proposals made by a

David Batts: a golfer invades the home of cricket.

review of MCC's management structure chaired by Sir Michael Jenkins, which had been set up after a series of management mistakes, such as serious cost overruns on projects such as the Media Centre. Interdepartmental rivalries – especially fraught between finance and marketing apparently – were compromising the quality of management. But Jenkins insisted that MCC hire someone who would bring commercial savvy to Lord's. He got his man.

When he applied for the job, Batts had no experience of running a sporting venue of any kind. He was from the hotel trade, having run a smart, upmarket group called Edwardian Hotels. He had also chaired the London Tourist Board for three years. He had not been on the list of candidates provided by the headhunters commissioned by MCC, but, having applied for the job by answering a newspaper advertisement, he eased his way on to the shortlist of six.

The selection committee was composed of two distinguished City bankers – Jenkins, then MCC treasurer, and Oliver Stocken, the chairman of finance – plus Roger Knight, whose deputy Batts would be. They warmed to Batts's experience, his energy, and his way of expressing himself; 'He was very enthusiastic. That mattered. He really wanted to do the job,' says Stocken. Also, Batts was in his mid-fifties, a near contemporary of Knight, so he would not be competing for the top job. A couple of candidates who had been experienced chief executives themselves were rejected because they might not have fitted into a small group of managers who were beholden to lay committees.

Batts is a salesman: he is glad-handed, has a ready smile and exudes energy and confidence. His focus was on the paying customers, who had for decades suspected that they were admitted to MCC's ground only on sufferance. 'I realised that we didn't talk about customers. They never got on our radar. It was all right if you were a member or a corporate guest, but if you were Joe Public, no one was paying any attention to your needs.'

Batts was pushing at an open door. The key word in the developing language of MCC was now 'branding'. New stands were making the ground a better place to look at and to sit in, but the old image of old men snoozing in the sun was slow to fade. The marketing men denounced Father Time as a symbol of 'Old Lord's'. New Lord's would de-emphasise MCC, and concentrate on Lord's itself. It was renamed 'The Home of Cricket'. The name became the brand. By 2003, the down-stroke of the L had become three stumps to emphasise that this was a cricket ground, not a private club. 'Gubby' Allen would have been turning in his grave.

Branding was the language Batts understood, and evidence of it was soon to be seen in the signage. Direction signs were decorated with remarks made about Lord's by famous cricketers. (Keith Miller: 'Every time I walk up those sprig-scarred steps of the Pavilion, I know I am in the very same footsteps as W. G. Grace.') Banners were hung from the back of the Compton and Edrich stands celebrating great performances at Lord's, such as Graeme Smith's 259 in 2003 and Glenn McGrath's 8 for 38 in 1997.

Previously, public notices in the ground had always emphasised the things spectators could not do. Batts came from a trade with utterly different priorities. 'My background was all about customers, and it was evident to me that there was a lot to do.' A survey indicated that improvements could start with the gatemen, doormen and stewards. Some of them were celebrated for their officious bad manners. Even senior committee men are sometimes startled by the brusque way they are met on arrival. Sunil Gavaskar had been refused entry at the North Gate because he forgot his membership pass, and the gateman reported that he was the sixth 'Sunil Gavaskar' to attempt to gain admittance that day. Another story, perhaps apocryphal, tells of the great Olympic middle-distance gold-medallist and MP Sebastian Coe arriving at a gate at the back of the Pavilion, where he was told by the gateman that his name was not on his list. 'My name is Coe,' he said, 'Sebastian Coe.'

'Well, it won't take you long to run round to the right gate then,' replied the gateman.

Gatemen were sent to charm school, and most became charming and helpful, although a couple of them must have failed their exams. In a recent

VIEW FROM THE GRAND STAND: *'Wednesday 17th August 2005 – It's the second day of the Frizzell County Championship match between Middlesex and Sussex, and frustratingly for the home team Sussex is accumulating a lot of runs. I feel very privileged today as I have the whole of the upper Grand Stand completely to myself and wow – what a view. And with the warm and sunny weather, I know I'd rather be up here than the poor batsman down there encircled by the looming opposition…'*

survey of spectators at Lord's both gatemen and stewards scored well. Stewards are a separate case. They lack the authority of the gatemen, many are pensioners, and they have less weight to throw around, even if they cared to do so. A few are robust figures brought in on major match days to deal with pitch invasions, but most are kindly figures whose greatest problem is enforcing the rule that forbids the use of mobile phones in the stands.

I have watched a steward trying to dissuade an Indian spectator from using his mobile – the steward was an Indian too, which helped. 'Why not?' asked the spectator, faintly incredulous. 'Because this is the Marylebone Cricket Club,' the steward replied quietly. The phone was switched off. Some rules of crowd behaviour at Lord's probably could not be applied elsewhere: banning of blaring horns and big flags, for example. At first blush, these rules appear to be an intrusion on a spectator's freedom, but principles of individual liberty come under intolerable strain if you are sitting next to a banner-waving, horn-blowing fanatic.

Consumer surveys suggested that gatemen were a minor irritation compared to the food. They told MCC what it already knew: the consumers thought the food they bought was of poor quality, especially at the price.

There was not much Batts could do about that. Until the end of the 2004 season, all the catering on the ground had been contracted out to Sodexho, a French multinational, which also feeds Epsom Racecourse and the US Marines. Annual turnover from catering was £5m – 70 per cent from sales at matches, 30 per cent from banqueting – and, in return for the catering rights, Lord's got a cheque for £1m. Batts's problem was that visitors to Lord's were not his customers, but Sodexho's. The only way to achieve a direct relationship with those customers, which he wanted, was to take the catering in-house.

It was a formidable challenge. Take one example: on big match days one thousand catering staff are hired to cook, serve and wash up. There is a pool of them in London during the summer, moving between Lord's, Wimbledon and Ascot. Many are capable Poles and Czechs, but a nice smile and a willing attitude would not be enough for Batts: 'If you're paying £70 a head for food and drink in a box, you get pretty hacked off if you've got a waiter who can't make a gin and tonic.' He does not suffer from lack of confidence: 'With my background, Lord's have someone with experience. I understand the economies of catering, and I'm not frightened.' The committee was reassured by Batts's advice that, while management would be a heavy responsibility, the risk was slight and the potential profit was tempting. If it didn't work, a contract caterer such as Sodexho would bid for a new contract, he advised. 'The committee was concerned about quality,' Batts reports. 'The food has always been awful. Even if we didn't make any more money, that would be all right as long as we got the quality right.'

First on the agenda was the main kitchen in the Tavern Banqueting Suite that sits above the pub by the Grace Gates. Upgrading, at a cost of £350,000, was unavoidable. 'The dishwasher didn't work half the time,' says Batts. The bar in the Tavern Stand would be completely rebuilt. A good deal of the food would be freshly prepared in the ground, and some would be provided by selected concessionaires. Batts had hoped Pret A Manger would provide the sandwiches. When they declined, it was decided that Lord's' own team of ten would make sandwiches and baguettes. (Pret A Manger's recipes are on the net.) Cornish pasties would come from the West Cornish Pasty Company. For the Harris Garden behind the Pavilion, Batts did a deal with Simon Parker Bowles of Green's, a fashionable watering hole in St James's, to provide breakfast, lunch and tea, with the emphasis on smoked salmon, and scones. Curries would come from Tamarind of Mayfair and the *Good Food Guide*. Picnic hampers were to be provided by Carluccio's, the Italian delicatessen chain.

As for coffee ('absolutely disgusting'), it would be brewed in eight cappuccino machines. 'The only problem is the time it takes. It's like ice cream: people don't mind paying 50p more if it's good.' This belief of Batts lay at the heart of the new policy: food and drink at Lord's was not going to be cheap. It might cost more than the Sodexho product, but this food was intended to be a major part of a memorable day out. The assumption is that spectators who have paid £52 for a seat in a public stand are not going to quibble about spending a few pounds extra here and there. Lord's now reflects the prosperity of its audience. The ambition was to make Lord's an equal of Wimbledon, Ascot, even the opera at Glyndebourne.

The pub is a symbol of the New Lord's. For decades, spectators stood in front of the old Tavern, watching the cricket and drinking beer. It was a place to stroll and chat to friends. That stopped abruptly when the Tavern Stand was built. The rebuilt pub was on the other side of the Grace Gates, where it remained a local, catering for a noisy overflow on to the pavement on Test match days. The pub was held by tenants, and when their lease expired in the winter of 2004, MCC decided to rebrand it. Batts wanted to see the character of the Tavern change completely. A start was made with the food, but the old guard of regulars, known to Batts for 'rolling their own and watching the football', stayed put. The solution was no smoking and no football. Before long, most of those customers had gone elsewhere. The Tavern's day-to-day business concentrated more on food and wine, and, to eradicate unseemly behaviour on the pavement during Test matches, it was to be closed to the drinking public then, and devoted to corporate hospitality instead. The original idea was that drinking after close of play would be catered for inside the ground, out of sight of the neighbours. Unfortunately the Metropolitan Police did not approve, and the plan was dropped.

Drink is the real earner, of course. Batts proposed a fresh start, but when brewers were asked to make offers, the contract did not go to the highest bidder – who was thought by MCC to be more at home at football. It went to Scottish Courage, which meant Fosters, backed up by Kronenburg, though Kronenburg would not be served in public bars because it was considered too strong for mass consumption. Lager beer outsells bitter by four to one, but the prominent advertising hoardings for London Pride around the perimeter of the ground suggested, correctly, that its beers could also be bought there, in competition with Young's.

Beer prices would rise, but Batts was understanding about this: brewers were investing large sums in multi-pour machines, which can pour six pints in three seconds. The machines are from Australia, where beer-drinking technology is way ahead of anywhere else in the world. Batts had learned a useful lesson from the full house at the Twenty20 game between Middlesex and Surrey the previous summer. In the time it took to buy a beer, two overs were bowled – one-tenth of a whole innings. Intolerably long. Veuve Cliquot was to become the Lord's champagne, though there would be an 'own brand', as at Tesco's. Wolf Blass, the reliable Australian winemaker, was to supply the house wines, and Bibendum the quality stuff. A wide range of decent wines was promised for the major match days.

An optimist by nature, Batts budgeted for an increase of 25 per cent in the profit from catering – from £1m to £1.25m. The investment in new kitchens would be paid for out of cash, and if taking the catering in-house proved too much of a burden, MCC could subcontract again, with higher revenues attracting a higher price. It was hard to refuse a scheme which seemed to allow MCC to have its cake and eat it.

But Batts did not get an entirely free run with his drive for greater efficiency and higher profits. Roger Knight keeps his eye on the balance between cricket and commerce: 'There are three aspects to Lord's; one's cricket, another's the membership, but underpinning both is commercial reality. The moment commerce gets level with the other two or above them, then we're in danger.'

Knight was defining a balancing act, one that would become trickier now that Lord's was for caterers as well as cricketers.

SELLING THE TICKETS

No marketing wizard is required to sell tickets for the Ashes Test at Lord's. 'We'd sell out in days if it were open season,' says Simon Wakefield, a cheerful, plump figure wearing an MCC tie, who started work in the ticket office eighteen years ago and now runs it. Of people who work at Lord's he says: 'You either stay a while or you're out in a couple of years.' He still gets a buzz when he turns up at 6.30 a.m. on the first morning of a Test. The ticket office lies behind the Museum and though they can hear the crowd, they have to rely on TV for the score. There is a staff of eight; Wakefield claims it is the largest of its kind in the country and it handles applications for more than 300,000 tickets a year. His busiest period is when you would least expect it – from October to March, when Test cricket is being played thousands of miles away in the southern hemisphere, but MCC members and devotees of England are buying tickets for the following summer.

If MCC said 'first come, first served', as they do at all the other Test grounds – where the Ashes Tests were literally sold out in the autumn of 2004 – they would be vulnerable to exploitation by people they disapprove of. Wakefield's boss, MCC's assistant secretary Colin Maynard, says: 'If we were to sell on demand then the tours and bucket shops would blitz the system, and swallow up the tickets.' He leaves unspoken the consequence of selling on demand, which is that a supply of tickets would end up with touts on the black market. MCC does not tolerate touts.

In 2005, you could give tickets away for the first Test against Bangladesh, which was to take place at the end of May. Indeed, they did so, thousands of them, to schoolchildren. Because the Bangladeshi team has such poor results in Test cricket, persuading a good crowd to watch them at Lord's could be seen either as a burden or an opportunity, but Charles Fry's visit to Dhaka the previous winter had reinforced MCC's feeling that it must try to make Bangladesh's first Lord's Test a memorable occasion. The MCC Committee endorsed a management decision to maximise attendance rather than revenue. Wakefield was given targets: he should aim to have the ground a little more than half full, with 14,000 on the first day, 17,000 on the second and around 15,000 on the Saturday. One helpful decision was to tell people who had qualified for most of the boxes for the Ashes Test that they must also take one for the Bangladesh Test too. The joke among the pessimists at Lord's was that there might be more people in the boxes than anywhere else.

MCC already had experience of corralling a few thousand school-children for the first day of an unfashionable Test. Reaching London's Bangladeshi community though, was uncharted territory. They soon learned that most Bangladeshis were cash buyers who preferred to turn up on the day. Wakefield would have to be pro-active. MCC arranged with a Bangladeshi bank to sell tickets at its East End branch. Local councillors were courted, and a poster campaign was planned. They hoped to sell 3,000 tickets for each of the first two days. It was an ambitious target.

But demand for the Ashes Test is overwhelming, far greater that the capacity of the ground. A full house at Lord's would fill less than one-third of the seats in the Melbourne Cricket Ground (the MCG is also built for Australian Rules football finals, which sell out easily). Lord's could proba-bly sell 100,000 tickets for each of the first three days of an Ashes Test, but to expand to sell that many seats once every four years when the Aussies are here would be rather like creating enough generating capacity to supply the whole of Britain during the worst of cold spells. Even if there were enough space, seriously expanding the capacity would be much too expensive.

Besides, it would change the character of the place: a cricket ground would become a sports stadium.

Consequently, MCC has a complicated ballot for tickets – no more than a pair for each applicant this Ashes summer – based on a strict hierarchy of applicants, with MCC members at the top and Joe Public at the bottom. The system is designed to make as many people successful as supply and demand allows. Tickets are priced between £26 and £52 (children get in for £12), compared to £18 and £42 in 2001 – though higher prices never seem to reduce demand. There are 150,000 names on Simon Wakefield's mailing list, which goes out to the members and associate members first, at the beginning of November. 'Like Wimbledon, we think a ballot is the fairest way,' says Wakefield. The chances for anyone without a place in the pecking order are better than for a win in the lottery, but not a lot.

The exact capacity of Lord's is harder to calculate than you might imagine. Wakefield gets as close to a reliable figure as he can through a process of elimination. He starts with a seating capacity of 28,000 – though that can rise to 30,000 if more members turn up at the gate than they expect. First deduct 1,500 seats behind the sight screen: no view, no sale. We're down to 26,500. First to be served are MCC members whose membership card includes tickets for each day's play at the Test. If they all turned up, the ground would already be two-thirds full, but only about half of them do so. Wakefield's 'educated punt' is that 9,000 members and guests will want a place in the Pavilion, or the Warner, Allen and Tavern Stands that flank it, on the first three days at least. (A record 6,008 members attended on the second day of the 2001 Ashes Test.) That leaves 17,500 seats. On the top tier of the Grand Stand, 1,106 seats are owned by debenture holders. They have to say whether or not they propose to use their seat; most do, but Wakefield sells them if they do not. Say the total remaining falls by 1,000, to 16,500. On that same tier 700 seats are allocated to Keith Prowse and Peter Parfitt Sports, ticket agencies that have long-term arrangements with Lord's. Fewer than 16,000 are left now. At the top of the Mound Stand, 536 more seats are spoken for by debenture holders; and each of the 70 boxes has an allocation of eighteen tickets. Together, that is just short of 2,000 seats, which takes the remaining capacity below 14,000. Another 1,000 seats are gobbled up by the ECB and npower, the series sponsor. Then take away 413 seats with restricted views – some behind TV cameras. Out of our original 28,000, the number of tickets for sale to people who enter the ballot is 12,415.

First in the ballot are MCC members buying tickets for friends. They could sell the whole ground to members, Wakefield says. Next in the hierarchy are associate members, then candidates for membership, followed by members of county clubs. There is an allocation for members of the Melbourne Cricket Club, and, in an Ashes summer, a batch of tickets is reserved for Australian tour groups. In mid-December, when those allocations have been filled, punters get the rest. Colin Maynard outlines MCC policy: 'We always keep what we describe as a decent number of seats for the general public, a few thousand a day.' The final number of general sales is affected by the number of debenture seats that come on the market. In 2005, planning permission was finally granted for the construction of two temporary stands behind the Compton and Edrich Stands, which can seat a further 600 or so spectators.

Wakefield's office dealt with almost three times as many applications as there were tickets available for the Ashes Test: 20,000 came in the mail and 15,000 via the internet. Demand for the second day was so great that no member received more than one Rover ticket. The computer system, which was introduced two years ago, scans every application and turns each one round in 72 hours. Wakefield loves his new IT system, and is especially keen on internet booking. He and his colleagues can organise applications on the screen and conduct the ballot by choosing names at random. Postal applications are piled high on shelves in the office. The successful applications are plucked from these piles and routed to the ticket desk where one machine prints the tickets and a second produces a receipt. No more tearing tickets out of paper books. The address on the receipt fits neatly behind the window in a plain white envelope. 'That's to guard against theft,' says Wakefield.' The problem of tickets stolen in the post office became so bad a few years ago that, to foil the thieves, the staff would take piles of envelopes to post on their way home at pillar boxes in different postal addresses.

Australians on tour parties are a special case. A tour operator clearly enhances the value of his package if he can guarantee tickets. One of them offered Wakefield a 50 per cent premium on the face price of tickets in return for a monopoly of the tickets reserved for Australian visitors. 'We stuck to our guns,' says Wakefield. Counting individual applications and tour parties together, there were 1,500 applications from Australians for the first day, and 1,300 for the second – including members of the Melbourne and Sydney Cricket Clubs which have reciprocal membership with MCC. Even tour companies had to make individual applications for their customers, and these were accompanied by a passport number. To make absolutely sure the tickets ended up in the right hands, MCC required the lucky ones to produce their passports when they collected their tickets at Lord's on the eve of the Test.

A few Australians thought they knew a clever way of acquiring scarce tickets. They wrote to their old pal Tom Graveney, and asked for help. Graveney is host in the President's Box each day during the Test but the majority of his guests comes from provisional lists of VIPs and former cricketers prepared by Stephanie Lawrence. 'I tick the ones I want to see,' he says. His personal allocation is just two tickets a day, so he was no help to those anxious Aussies.

When all the tickets had been allocated, Wakefield broke down the sale of seats in the public stands for the second day of the Ashes Test to show who got what, and he found that 1,026 had gone overseas, mainly to Australia, which represents 5 per cent of 18,782 seats with good views. MCC members had got 21 per cent, associates and candidates 10 per cent, which meant, once the members in their own stands and the friends were included, just half the ground's capacity would be swallowed by MCC itself. County members had received 11 per cent. Hospitality companies took 8 per cent, as did the ECB and npower, the Test sponsors, and the debenture holders. 667 seats had restricted views, and 800 were unsaleable because they had no view at all.

Members of the general public, who are gloomy because Lord's seems like a closed shop for Ashes Tests, had done rather better than they expected. The allocation was 4,002 seats, or 20.58 per cent precisely.

Each ticket is numbered and can be traced. The purchaser of any ticket that appears on the internet auction house eBay, in the personal columns of the posh papers, or at the entrance to St John's Wood station can be identified, and, unless he has a very good excuse, will be shamed by the club (Maynard reports that, in the past decade, three members have been hauled over the coals). 'First come, first served' policies, like those at the other Test grounds, are convenient and profitable, but the other clubs appear not to worry much that many of the tickets will make their way on to the black market. MCC adopts a higher moral tone. By emphasising fairness, they reject a free market in tickets. The inference is that people who buy on the black market are jumping the queue, and there is something distasteful about profiting by selling a ticket at more than the face price. This attitude reflects the predominantly English, male, and middle-class make-up of MCC.

No one in the hierarchy at MCC was amused when a pair of Ashes Test tickets turned up on eBay early in the spring of 2005. Since the numbers were legible, Wakefield's office traced the original applicant in no time at all. Confronted by MCC, he said they were indeed his tickets, but his wife, who knew they must be worth something, had put them up at auction. Since they fetched seven times their face price, she was both very right and very wrong.

THE LITTLE RED BOOK

Men and women who want to become members of MCC need a proposer and a seconder, but what they need most is patience – except for women, for whom it was impatience that was required until the male monopoly was finally breached in 1998. At the start of 2005, there were 9,098 names on the waiting list – 397 of them women, or ladies, as they are known by MCC. Since there were only 429 vacancies in 2004, this suggests a waiting period of 21 years and 8 months. There is one back door, and Tom Graveney passed through it in 1972. His qualification was his style and his record as a Test cricketer. The dismal circumstances of the end of his Test career were ignored by him and MCC, and he became an honorary life member.

The number of members increased from 16,000 to 18,000 in 1976, but the desirability of membership has risen even more sharply. The computerised record in the membership office tells me I had waited for only sixteen years when I became a full member in 1998; now, it would take five or six years longer than that. Cricket-lovers who have not managed to play for England, and who do not qualify as playing members, will be lucky if they are elected before they reach middle age. It is no surprise that the average age of an MCC member is 58.

The length of time it now takes to join is a recipe for an ageing membership. At some stage, candidates are offered Associate Membership. There are 4,000 of these and they may use the Pavilion and the members' stands on all but the most popular match days. The list of members is completed by 204 senior members, who pay a reduced subscription in return for fewer privileges.

Women have been members since 1999. To pre-empt the criticism that the only privilege sexual equality would bring was a place at the bottom of the long waiting list, 22 honorary lady life members and 23 full lady playing members were then elected. But this tiny minority is not without a voice. In 2004 Rachael Heyhoe Flint, a slight but formidable figure who had captained England's women from 1966 to 1977, was elected to the MCC Committee; she already sat on the Marketing and Cricket Committees.

The length of waiting time is dictated by disenchantment and death. Resignations normally number between 100 and 120 each year, though the keeper and student of the lists, Michael Capitelli, who manages the membership office, notes that there are always fewer resignations during an Ashes summer. In 2004 271 deaths, 87 lapsed members and 62 resignations created 420 vacancies. To these already sitting in the Pavilion, the average annual death rate of 1.5 per cent seems like quite enough. For those down the waiting list, it sounds horribly low.

When they are finally elected – a few candidates are blackballed, but it is very rare – members get a London cricket-lovers' freedom pass – a little red book measuring 4 inches by 2.75 inches, Inside the back cover is a plastic card with a photograph of the member (still called 'Esq.'). It lists the summer's fixtures, useful telephone numbers such as 'prospects of play', and a stern injunction against the use of mobile telephones – in the Pavilion at all times and in the rest of the ground when the umpires are on the field (clubmen generally feel strongly about mobiles). Then come fourteen pages of admission vouchers: ten for two Test matches, two for one-day internationals, a Twenty20 cup match and the Cheltenham and Gloucester Trophy Final.

A subscription to MCC costs £324 for a London, or inner town member; £270 for an outer town member and £161 for country members, school staff, and under-30s – to make the subscription less costly for active playing members. Judged solely in terms of match tickets, it is a bargain. Tickets for two Tests lasting five days each at £52 a time would more than cover the cost. Of course, very few members spend that much time at Lord's, though Mick

IN THE TURRET:
'Saturday 28th August 2004.
So here I am sat in one of the
turrets of the Lord's Pavilion at
Lord's Cricket Ground, with a
crowd of around 23,000, all here
to watch the Cheltenham and
Gloucester Trophy Final between
Worcestershire and Gloucestershire.
This beautiful, listed Pavilion
will be restored and refurbished
in a couple of weeks.'

Hunt, the head groundsman, declares that there is a small band of members so dedicated that it would turn up on Christmas Day if the ground were open. Until three years ago, the subscription was an even better bargain. Then it went up by one-third, at a stroke, principally to pay for ground improvements, and that produced convincing evidence that the members think they are getting a fair deal. There were isolated cries of pain, but very few resignations.

Michael Capitelli, who is in charge of producing the little red membership book in time for each new season, was celebrating 30 years at Lord's in 2005. He says he has watched Lord's change (new stands), and stay the same (jackets, ties and acceptable footwear in the Pavilion). He joined the staff straight from school. His family assumed he was bound for a white-collar job in a bank or the Civil Service. But his father had taken him to Lord's in 1965 when he was a boy and two years later he had been among the TV audience for Graveney's brilliant 151 against the Indian spinners. He loved cricket, and when MCC offered him a clerical post, he didn't think twice. He declares that his decision was justified later that summer when he met Geoff Boycott.

Capitelli keeps the waiting list in order, makes sure the eight per cent of members who won't do direct debit pay up by 1 March at the latest, and informs new members that they are also required to stump up a £540 entrance fee. But the busiest time of the year – as with the ticket office – is in the winter, when he prepares and sends out 18,000 little red books, each with the correct photograph on the plastic card inside the back cover. They take two months to prepare, and there are various irritants along the way. Capitelli can't complete the text until he gets the fixture list, which is due on 18 November, but is always late. Between mid-November and mid-April he has a staff of four. 'Nobody else understands how much work is involved. It's taken for granted to be honest with you,' he says.

The booklets are finally printed in Nuneaton at a cost of £2 each, and the reason why Capitelli sometimes feels taken for granted is that his system works smoothly. That is his reward. 'I see the members waving their red passes at the gateman and I think, my department sent those out.'

A SPARKLING ICON

Tom Graveney stands on the half-landing of the staircase in the Lord's Museum looking down, a little nervously, at a crowd of MCC members jostling in a confined space. It is 8 April, and he is to perform an agreeable Presidential duty: the formal reopening of the Pavilion, which has been extensively refurbished during the winter. It turns out to be a splendid example of his Presidential style. A speech has been written for him, of course; it is thirteen short paragraphs in length and a blameless piece of work intended to thank some of the people who had supervised the work. 'My Lords, ladies and gentlemen, welcome to Lord's,' it begins. Graveney dutifully sticks to the script for the first sentence before looking up to add: 'It's not a great morning, is it? I think you've done absolutely fantastically to come to listen to me speak.' It is drizzling outside and there is only a slim chance of play in the first game of the 2005 season, between MCC and Warwickshire, the Champion County.

He reads the next sentence: 'The Pavilion, now a Grade II star listed building, was built during the winter of 1889–90.' And then he looks up: 'Just being in the Pavilion is one of the great things that happens to any cricketer. Walk through the Long Room, you get the polite applause, the warm welcome as you walk down the ground, to bat or bowl . . . when you get nought, and this happened to me once or twice, you walk back and it's a little cool, but there are always some nice people who say, "Bad luck, son, better luck next time." Playing at Lord's is very special. It's the best ground in the world . . . It's the fairest ground; our crowds are so cosmopolitan. Every single cricketer wants to come here, and I've been lucky – I've played here a few times.' His spectacles case falls to the floor. 'Another one down,' he says.

He takes the audience into his confidence. 'The Executive Board, we start our meetings at 8.30 a.m. We were invited to have a look, only six or seven weeks ago. It was like a bombsite and I remember thinking as I walked out, we're never going to get this done' – a deft introduction to thanking the architects, the project managers, and the contractors. He thanks the Arts and Library Committee, the Estates Committee and David Batts, the deputy chief executive, who was MCC's man in charge ('he's a man with a knack of getting on with people').

He confesses that he has not seen the restored building yet and asks the audience to follow him across to the Pavilion. Then, an afterthought: 'It's

A rare sight: inside the Long Room during play.
Michael Vaughan, 'better luck next time'.

The handwritten text around the border of the illustration reads:

Sunday August 28th 2005, Its the National Village Cricket championship final between the two very fine teams of Sheriff Hutton Bridge from Yorkshire and Eynsford from Kent. You could not ask for a more perfect late summer's day no real contrast to four days earlier when the rain would not relent for the Thomas Lord match — such is the English summer. Anyway, what a great match today to complement the weather, entertaining, exciting, and closely fought and thoroughly enjoyable...

THE NATIONAL VILLAGE CHAMPIONSHIP:
'Sunday August 28th 2005. It's the National Village Final between the two very fine teams of Sheriff Hutton Bridge from Yorkshire and Eynsford from Kent. You could not ask for a more perfect late summer's day – a real contrast to four days earlier when the rain would not relent for the Thomas Lord match – such is the English summer. Anyway, what a great match today to complement the weather, entertaining, exciting and closely fought and thoroughly enjoyable…'

funny, you know. I've just had a thought. I'm a total right-hander, except in two things. When I batted, the left hand was my guide. I held the bat at the top and it swung back straight and came down straight. The other problem is that when I have a pair of scissors in my hand, I'm left-handed. So I hope they've got a left-handed pair of scissors over there.'

Left-handed or not, Tom Graveney held the scissors in his left hand to cut a red and yellow ribbon across the doorway and led a small crowd of members inside for a glass of champagne. Later that morning he confessed that he had woken during the night, worrying about the speech. He had no cause to. A light touch, instinctive modesty and experience of playing the game were the ingredients for a speech that must have been what Charles Fry had been hoping for from the new President.

The Pavilion was already more than a hundred years old when Westminster Council compelled MCC to live up to the building's distinguished architectural and historical status. The Pavilion had not been on the agenda of the Estates Committee, which looks after the fabric of Lord's. In the mid-1990s, the committee was preoccupied by the Media Centre, which had to be ready for the World Cup in spring 1999. The aluminium pod was the most radical structure MCC had ever contemplated, and no one at MCC had realised that it would present them with formidable problems involving both engineering and finance.

The Estates Committee was concerned about getting planning consent from Westminster Council and it orchestrated a shrewd public relations campaign to confront bureaucratic resistance. It worked. The Royal Fine Arts Commission had no objections. English Heritage worried away about the impact on views from Regent's Park, but raised no objection. Planning permission was applied for in September 1996, and granted, amazingly promptly, in November 1996.

But the planners added a condition that had nothing to do with the Media Centre: existing commentary boxes in the turrets on each side of the Pavilion must be removed and the areas left vacant should be returned to their original use as seating for members. BBC's Test Match Special was disgruntled at having to leave its privileged position above the visitors' dressing room, and threatened to stay put. They never thought to blame Westminster Council's planners.

MCC clearly had to do something. The question was, how much? The Media Centre soon became a celebrated, prize-winning architectural landmark, but the Estates Committee took plenty of time before deciding that, after devoting the best part of two decades to making Lord's more comfortable for paying spectators, MCC members deserved a treat, and there was no more deserving object than their clubhouse: the Pavilion.

Lord's Pavilion, built of red brick and terracotta, was designed by Thomas Verity, a distinguished theatre architect in the late-nineteenth century. He was involved in the terracotta detailing of the Royal Albert Hall, and he designed the Criterion Restaurant and Theatre, both still open for business daily in Piccadilly Circus, each a delightful conceit of decorative tiles and show business flair. He must have had a sense of humour, too: the fine terracotta heads that decorate the wall behind the first balcony are thought to be modelled on members of the MCC Committee of the time; individually, they look stern, puckish and bemused.

Verity was expert in buildings designed for an audience that wanted a good view, rooms where they could relax in good company and decent food and drink, ideally in well-designed surroundings. Verity met these requirements, and the builders began their work in the autumn of 1889. They completed it only nine months later. Much of the £21,000 cost was met by a loan from William Nicholson, of Nicholson's Gin, who had played at Lord's for Harrow and for the Gentlemen against the Players. Later, he became MCC President. The colours on the label of a bottle of Nicholson's Gin were red and yellow. Glenys Williams, the archivist in MCC Museum, believes that this gin bottle is the most likely inspiration for the club colours. Very apt.

After the Committee had formally approved the Estates Committee's proposal in April 2003, the plan was to vacate the building on 1 September 2004 and to return in the middle of March 2005. Costs had risen dramatically:

74

£21,000 in 1889–90 for the whole building had become £8.2m in 2004–05 just for the restoration, and that was after £1.05m had already been spent on preparatory work on the roof. Some members of MCC's own establishment thought the plans were unnecessarily ambitious, but the committee and the members, when they were consulted, were overwhelmingly in favour. The specification for the architects, engineers and builders was to conserve the fabric, to restore it where necessary, but not to stop there. They were encouraged to improve the grand old building wherever they could. Opportunities presented themselves in some unexpected places.

Maurice de Rohan became chairman of the Estates Committee at a tricky moment. Construction was well under way, costs for the Media Centre were out of control, and serious engineering problems remained unresolved. MCC needed an expert to take over the project, and turned to de Rohan. He does not appear so until he starts to talk, but de Rohan is an Australian with a distant French forebear. He is also the Agent-General for South Australia in London, representing the State in Britain and Europe. De Rohan is a small, energetic, jolly man who ran, with some partners, thriving architectural and engineering practices in Adelaide, Melbourne, New York and London, where he settled in the mid-1970s. He also follows cricket with an Australian's attention to detail and optimism about the result.

De Rohan's golden rule is 'Good clients make good buildings.' He learned the lesson as a practising engineer, and he was now applying it as the client. A good client knows what he wants, and does not change his mind about fundamentals after the job has begun. When his committee got down to business, it already had a template: a conservation plan had been prepared in 2001 by Donald Insall and Michael Shippobottom. That was a diagnostic history of the building, which identified what was original and what had been added, or taken away, and it itemised the areas that needed to be restored. The conservation plan gave the five architects' practices competing for the job a clear idea of what would be required. None of them was quite as famous as Sir Michael Hopkins (the Mound Stand) or Sir Nicholas Grimshaw (the Grand Stand). These were specialists in conservation. The

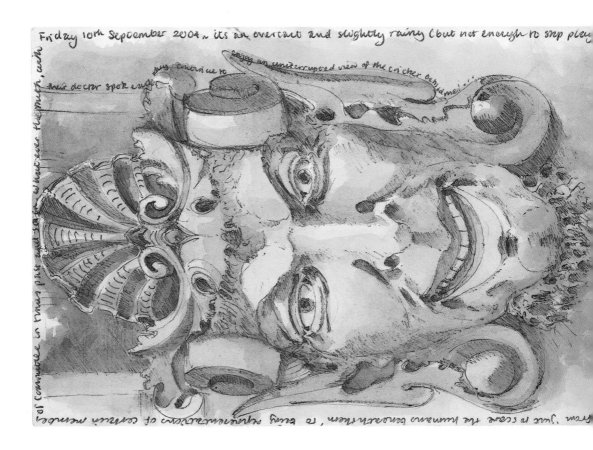

job went to a tall, slim, fastidious-looking man called Patrick Ettwein, who had learned his craft in the practice of Sir Basil Spence, the designer of the new Coventry Cathedral. His firm, Ettwein Bridges, had worked on the Houses of Parliament and the Law Society building.

The brief for the sympathetic restoration of the Pavilion was to strip out all the services and replace them, to hack away all the plaster in the basement and to look for extra office space. The turrets would be restored and a new viewing platform built on the flat roof behind the balcony seats at the top of the Pavilion. New inset lighting in the ceilings, a new heating system, lifts, kitchens and electrical services would be installed, all without altering the character of the Pavilion. This was functional architectural work; Ettwein calculated that if all the drawings were spread out, they would cover

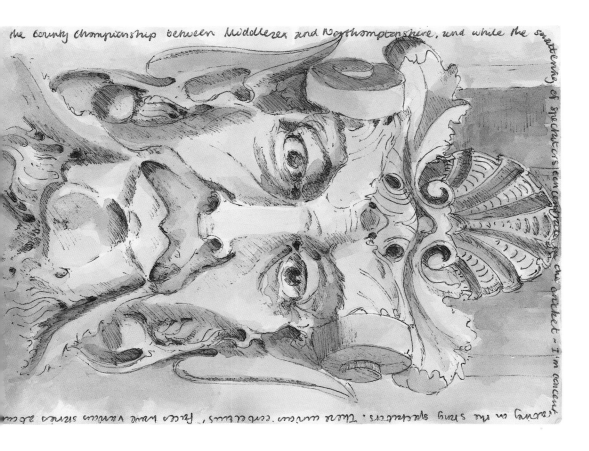

TERRACOTTA HEADS: *'Friday September 10th 2004 – it's an overcast and slightly rainy (but not enough to stop play) day for the County Championship match between Middlesex and Northamptonshire, and while the smattering of spectators concentrate on the cricket, I'm concentrating on the stony spectators. These curious 'corbellius' faces have various stories about them – from 'just to scare the humans beneath them' to being representations of certain members of committee in times past and so on. Whatever the truth, with their Doctor Spock ears they continue to enjoy an uninterrupted view of the cricket behind me!'*

the outfield. But what really interested him was the Long Room, the most important room in the building, not just because it is the largest – it is 93 feet from end to end, almost half as long again as a cricket pitch – but because it has so many uses. It is a viewing gallery, and a processional route from the dressing room to the wicket and back again. It is a banqueting hall on grand evenings, and a reception room for more informal occasions. It is an art gallery, and a lecture hall. Ettwein used it as a lecture hall to explain what he set out to do.

The conservation plan revealed details of the alterations made since 1890, and the good news was that most changes had been cosmetic. Two fireplaces on each side of the double door leading to the members' bar had been removed. The doors had been shut, though they remained intact. More significant architecturally was the patterned ceiling, which had been designed by Verity in the Queen Anne style he liked so well. It had fallen victim to the taste for the plain and functional in the 1950s, which had robbed the Long Room of much of its decorative charm. All was not lost, however, because the 1950s philistines had not attacked their own private preserve. The Committee Room at the south end of the Long Room retained its original ceiling, as did the Writing Room at the north end. Ettwein had a model to work from.

A company called Sames with long experience in restoration work was awarded the building contract, and they moved into the Pavilion on schedule on 1 September. The test would be whether they were ready to leave on 18 March, as scheduled. By the end of the 2004 cricket season, the back of the Pavilion was encased in scaffolding, and soon after that, the back and sides of the building disappeared behind the contractors' temporary blue wall. The façade was shrouded in plastic sheeting. Instead of ties and jackets, it was now hard hats that were compulsory.

Sames' contract manager was Stewart Harris, an obliging Scot who knew little about cricket. He took me on a conducted tour towards the end of October through what was then a building site. Wooden handrails and floors were protected by plastic sheets, and there were deep scars on the walls where old water pipe-work and electrical wiring had been stripped out. The basement corridors were deep in rubble from plaster that had been hacked off to reveal the original brick, but Harris knew exactly where the new ladies' lavatory would go. In the Long Room, the ceiling had completely disappeared behind what was known as birdcage scaffolding. Out of sight, builders were making vents for air extractors which would be cleverly hidden in the restored plasterwork pattern. Climbing the stairs, we could see a lift-shaft taking shape. On the balconies on each turret the terracotta decoration on the balustrades was being restored or replaced. On the roof, a vast Victorian water tank was being incorporated into the new roof terrace.

There were 67 workmen on the payroll at the time. Two of them from Australia had insisted on having their photograph taken in the visitors' dressing room. During the winter, the number would rise to 150, and English speakers became rarity. Lord's Pavilion was restored by skilled, hard-working craftsmen from Poland and Lithuania, who wanted as much work as they could get. There was plenty of it.

There are contingencies that neither client nor builders can foresee. In a lucky job, none arise; at Lord's one did, in the form of severe dry rot. Beams in the roof above the members' bar in the south turret and the south staircase outside it were so badly eaten away that they had to be stripped out. The faulty lead guttering that had let the water in had to be replaced. Harris estimated that this piece of bad luck put the project two to three weeks behind schedule. It was late in February, with six to seven weeks to go, when MCC's Executive Board were given a guided tour. Graveney wasn't exaggerating when he compared it to a bombsite in his speech.

Harris showed me round again not long afterwards, when some of the new features were emerging. In the basement, the ladies' lavatory was a riot of fine wood and black marble. A lavatory for the disabled had appeared and it was possible to discern the shape of the bar behind the newly opened doors to the Long Room. Painting had actually begun in the Committee Room. But the best moment in the gloom of late winter came when the scaffolding was removed from the Long Room ceiling and the delicate new plasterwork was exposed. It hid the sophisticated cooling system perfectly. 'That ceiling is the best part,' says de Rohan.

Those last seven weeks went by in a flurry of overtime work. Harris and a colleague toiled through the last weekend to clean the floors, and the building was handed over to MCC on 4 April. Strictly speaking, Harris was sixteen days behind schedule, but once he had exposed the dry rot, de Rohan and his colleagues were not inclined to criticise, especially as the total cost that winter was £7.06m compared to the original estimate of £8.2m. The £1.05m spent on preparatory work brought the final total to just under £8.2m, which would be paid out of cash revenues over three years.

There were still details to be finished, and staff and workmen wore blue plastic overshoes to protect the floors, but the curator could begin to re-hang the paintings, and staff could start moving back into their offices. The white paint on the balcony railings shone brightly through the murky weather. De Rohan had airily suggested that the doors on the balconies might be painted green and the railings yellow, wondering whether anyone would notice that these were the colours of his Australian cricket team. They all did.

After Tom Graveney cut the ribbon – with his left hand – members wandered through their new home. Some said it was so grand that they felt they were in an hotel. The hanging of the paintings was incomplete on the staircases, but was receiving much praise in the Writing Room, where the theme was Lord's itself. The Long Room had become a gallery of the history of cricket, though not everyone was persuaded by the inclusion of the one modern portrait (a group of three cricketers), intended to balance the three Victorian gentlemen who founded a club of touring players called I Zingari. Cricket's legends were not far away, in the bar behind the Long Room, where old favourites such as Keith Miller and Ian Botham would feel entirely at home.

It took a while before I spotted the Don. Sir Donald Bradman was to be found in the space between two doors at the entrance to the lift that leads to the bar. Any member holding the door for another would certainly miss the portrait of the greatest of all cricketers. Accident or design? Three plausible explanations were to be had, each containing a value judgement. Those who think it flattering to the Don say that, in the hierarchy of paintings first seen on entering the Pavilion, the first, on the right hand wall, is the Queen and Prince Philip, next is Lord's itself, then Bradman – third in the pecking order.

The second view of Bradman's position derives from Bodyline, the most heated episode in cricket history. Douglas Jardine, who led England to victory in Australia in 1932/33, had stared out from the walls of the Long Room until Ted Dexter declared that deliberately intimidating batsmen contradicted the Spirit of Cricket, and had poor Jardine packed off to the Museum. Would this injustice not have been exacerbated if the Don were in a more prominent position?

The third view is aesthetic: the painting is not a good one because it makes Sir Don look like a stockbroker (which he was, of course). So the placement was controversial, and it was going to be interesting to see whether Bradman stayed put.

Up on top of the building, decking had been laid on the turret roofs and on the terrace that lies between them – fresh wood, smart chairs, and a high view. It was a cold, wet day (lightning actually struck the roof above the south turret on this, the first day of the season). But members were enjoying the prospect of the roof on a warm day with a faint breeze. Not a bad spot for a short sleep after lunch.

The most astonishing innovation among the improvements was to be found in the upgrading of the men's lavatory in the basement. There was a good joke on the doors, one saying Out, the other Not Out, so as to direct the traffic. Marble and tiles in good taste greet the users, but the striking addition is of two flat-screen TVs, one just above the urinal, the other on the way out, to keep members informed of what was happening in the middle while they answered the call of nature. On the opening day, they were showing the Pope's funeral. Those TV screens could be interpreted as the ultimate attention to detail. They also indicate the adjective that best describes the new Pavilion: opulent.

A minority of members thought the refurbishment was over the top, but the initial reaction suggested that the majority would be delighted. They had only to look around them, before looking out on to the field of play, to feel even more privileged than they had done before.

HANDING ON

A president of MCC is expected to choose his successor late in the winter. Since he has served only half his term, this seems premature, but tradition dictates that the identity of the new President is announced at the annual general meeting, which in Tom Graveney's year was to be held on 4 May 2005. It would be MCC's 218th, no less. The MCC Committee had considered whether a one-man electorate was the proper way to conduct affairs, and had concluded 'the traditional nomination procedure has served the Club well over a great number of years.' New Lord's would let things be, and Tom Graveney would make the choice. But not before listening to advice.

Speculation began in the New Year; Graveney gave it no assistance at all: no winks, no nudges. He discussed the subject with Roger Knight early in January, and heard a number of ideas: 'If he wanted to choose his wife, he could do it – if she was a member. If there was a strong feeling that he was going in the wrong direction, I would certainly be prepared to say, "Look I just don't think that's going to work." Others will too,' said Knight. When he was President, Ted Dexter sent a list of five names to senior members of the committee and asked them to tick them in order of preference. The democratic choice was Sir Tim Rice.

Since Roger Knight was retiring in 2006, a top priority would be the choice of a new secretary and chief executive, so the new President would ideally be someone who was familiar with the club's internal politics, and trusted by insiders on the MCC Committee. Should it be a former Test cricketer, or an administrator, or a notable figure in the game? If he had been younger and fitter, John Woodcock, former cricket correspondent of *The Times* might well have appeared on the list; as a former trustee, he had impeccable credentials, but was disinclined to travel regularly from his home in Longparish, on the river Test in Hampshire (the 'Sage of Longparish' is the correct way to speak of him). Obviously, a distinguished figure like John Major would be mentioned. Graveney was a keen admirer, and Major had been a member of the MCC Committee, and would be re-elected in 2005. But Major was still a very busy man. He had time for the Committee, but he could not contemplate a time-consuming job like the Presidency. Not yet anyway.

It is customary for the name of the new President to be leaked to one of the papers a day or two before the annual meeting, but not in 2005. When I asked him earlier on the day to let me into the secret, all Graveney would say was that it would be a surprise, a pleasant surprise. But the name would not be revealed until the last item on the agenda, number nine.

The President's role at MCC has been curtailed by the new position of the Chairman, but he chairs the annual general meeting, and some recent predecessors had had a torrid time. Tony Lewis, for example, had been the victim of a vengeful minority – they hated having been asked to pay to watch the World Cup final. Graveney prepared carefully; his speech would contain none of the asides that had enlivened the Pavilion opening. He was required to mention some items; and for the questions that might arise under any other business, Graveney had a briefing book, just like the Prime Minister's at Question Time. He and Knight studied it together on the morning of the meeting.

It was another grey day at Lord's. Rain threatened, and the light was poor, but neither stopped an MCC team starting promptly in the annual match against MCC Young Cricketers. Most of the 22 had never played at Lord's, and they were not going to let a few spots of rain spoil the occasion.

The annual meeting takes place on the floor of the Indoor School. For an issue as controversial as the election of women members, it was packed. In 2005, when the sole contentious issue was the treatment of elderly members, it was not and many of those who did turn up were old enough to declare a personal interest. Graveney started as he proposed to go on: he said he didn't want to restrict anyone's right to speak, but suggested, in the nicest possible way, that, whatever the point, two to three minutes ought to be sufficient. Cue a murmur of cynical laughter. There were some familiar faces for whom three minutes had never been enough.

The Presidential speech was listened to attentively. He concentrated on cricket, reporting that MCC Universities gave MCC a clear operational role in English cricket for the first time since 1968. He was glad of it, he said, because he wanted MCC to be at the heart of 'our game'. But he was realistic enough to understand that what the audience cared most about was the level of their subscriptions, and tickets for the Ashes Test. He appreciated the disappointment of all the members who had not got the tickets they had applied for, and hoped they would be satisfied by an extra 600 seats for members in the Pavilion. Getting in was what exercised the members; keeping the wrong people out was the preoccupation of MCC's administrators. A paragraph in the Presidential speech registering deep distaste for members who had the gall to sell their tickets into the black market sounded more Maynard than Graveney.

He admitted that members would think he was ducking a bouncer if he did not touch on the contentious issue of life members who pay no subscription after they have been members for 50 years. The problem is that, with life expectancy rising fast, the number of life members could increase sharply, leaving a hole in subscription revenues. The committee proposed that members should agree to wait until they had clocked up 60 years before being entitled to free membership. Old men who were about to benefit under the old rule were understandably disenchanted, but even in this mature gathering they were in a minority of nearly two to one.

The scourge of MCC had some words to say about the subject. Michael Geliot, an opera producer from Wales, who wears his steel-grey hair long and has jet-black eyebrows, was a leading member of a reform group in the late 1990s. MCC's governance is an obsession with him, and each year he speaks at length about it. His eyebrows express extreme displeasure when he hears the subdued groan that accompanies his approach to the microphone. Although he was on the side of the elderly, what Geliot said he dislikes was members using their wealth to buy position at MCC. 'What do you want? Rich blighters or people who love cricket?' he cried. Clearly, the answer was that MCC wants members who love cricket and can also afford to pay the annual subscription until they are 75. It does not regard itself as a charitable institution.

The debate rarely involved cricket. One member did ask for appropriate recognition of Wally Hammond, who, he said, deserved better than an obscure spot in the Museum. Graveney jumped in: 'He was one of the greatest cricketers, the greatest I've ever seen. I'll do what I can to raise his profile.' The characteristics of the Graveney Presidency are tolerance towards members who want to speak, and patience for those who talk nonsense, or go on for too long.

Two and a quarter hours had passed before Graveney arrived at item number nine. Choosing his successor, he said, is one of the most important decisions a President must take. He dropped some clues: his man had played in the Eton v. Harrow match in 1947; he won Cambridge Blues; and was elected to MCC in 1955. He had played in 289 first-class games between 1951 and 1968. This was enough to create a buzz of speculation. Then Graveney revealed that his successor, when he was playing for Sussex, had spun him out many times. That clinched it. Even before he announced the name, it had to be Robin Marlar. The round of applause that followed the announcement reassured Graveney. Afterwards, Marlar stood in the central aisle smiling broadly as he received congratulations. Graveney had clearly done the right thing. Roger Knight thought so, with the mildest reservations: 'Robin's terrific. When he came on the MCC Committee, I thought "we need someone like this." He's a handful for the Chairman, he's bright, thinks things through. He's good, but he can be time consuming.'

Marlar's presidential qualifications start with his cricket. His record in the university match has rarely been equalled, and he took 970 wickets with his off-spin at 25.22 in first-class cricket. He would surely have played for England had his career not coincided with those of England's finest-ever array of off-spin bowlers – Jim Laker, Roy Tattersall, Bob Appleyard, Fred Titmus, David Allen and Ray Illingworth ('He didn't get a look-in,' Graveney recalls). Marlar was a controversialist known as 'Snarler'. This was not because of what he wrote as cricket correspondent of the *Sunday Times* – F. R. Brown, the former England captain and MCC President, gave him the name after hearing him appeal early in his career. It is not a name he likes. He was a committee man, elected to the MCC Committee in 1998 – with the support of Geliot's reform group – and is still an influential member of the Cricket Committee. He was a principal architect of the over-throw of the Sussex committee in 1999, and had just been elected President of his county club. In a business career he had been a headhunter, which ought to come in useful. Marlar was 74; he had two new hips and two new knees, and was still able to draw on a deep reserve of energy.

He remembers fondly having dismissed Graveney a few times early in both their careers before Graveney got used to him. Marlar said he thought that Graveney might have been guilty of playing the bowler and not the ball. It happens: a batsman thinks he knows what to expect from a bowler and plays accordingly. Mike Atherton, for example, played Glenn McGrath and not the ball. But Graveney was not impressed by the analysis, which offended his uncomplicated attitude to batting: 'I used to play every ball as it comes. Playing the bowler doesn't make sense to me. It's the ball that gives you the problem. They all bowl bad ones, and if you're thinking about the bowler, you'll miss it.'

When he talked later about his choice, Graveney could not remember who had first mentioned Marlar as a potential candidate. He and Marlar had not been close when they played county cricket, but that was not relevant: 'First and foremost from my point of view, he was a cricketer. The name came suddenly out of the blue. I'd been impressed with him at

Cricket Committee meetings. He's bright, and he puts things well. He'll be good for the club, and maybe a bit controversial.' He implied that this was not necessarily a bad thing. 'I rang him up and asked whether he would do me a favour. Would he become President? There was a silence for ten seconds. Then he said "It's the nicest phone call I've had in my life." He rang me up the following day and said, "Is it true, what you said last night?" '

When the truth had sunk in, and each of them was a guest of honour at the dinner on the evening of the annual meeting, Graveney reminded Marlar of a game at Cheltenham in which Marlar had employed a stultifying defensive strategy by bowling to eight men on the leg side when Sussex were losing. Graveney raised an eyebrow – as a reminder that this old man does not forget.

THE BANKER SPEAKS

The President does not get involved in MCC's finances unless he has a taste for budgets and cash flows. Tom Graveney was happy to leave the job to the experts. Oliver Stocken, the Treasurer, is an erect figure with black hair. He explained to me the current state of MCC's finances in the Mayfair offices of a firm of corporate-finance advisers. His job is to advise the advisers. In the entrance hall stands a larger than life-size figure, by the sculptor Elizabeth Frink, of a naked black man with a white face. Stocken remarks that it was very costly.

He is a City man, an accountant by training who worked at the merchant bankers N. M. Rothschild before joining Barclays, where he eventually became finance director. He is now in his early sixties and has a portfolio of non-executive directorships. In the boardroom power list produced by *The Times* Stocken ranks number three among the top one hundred. His news is that MCC's finances are in remarkably good shape.

Each year he presents the accounts to the annual general meeting in the form of a booklet. He refers me to the last page, where there are three core numbers. 'They show what we do to generate income, from subscriptions, major matches, hospitality, catering and from the shops. The second figure is our surplus, which we can use to reinvest in the ground. The third figure is members' funds, which shows how much we're worth.'

The figures show income of £16.4m. Two five-day Tests against New Zealand and West Indies, plus other major matches in 2004, raised £4.6m.

(The ECB earned £2.2m from two Lord's Tests.) Income from members' subscriptions was static at £4.3m, but areas such as advertising, boxes and hospitality and especially the retail activities showed healthy increases. The surplus before depreciation was £4.8m, and members' funds were £31.8m. 'If we suddenly needed £20 million, we'd probably be able to persuade a bank to lend it,' says Stocken.

Late in the 1980s, when MCC was in trouble and had borrowed up to the hilt at the bank, the finances were poorly managed. Sir Paul Getty bailed out the Mound Stand development, but there were serious cost overruns for the Media Centre and the Nursery Pavilion. What is the financial legacy of these bad times? What does MCC owe now?

Stocken refers to a table in his report. Debt in 2004 was £10.3m, down from £17.4m five years earlier. Of that, £7.5m is borrowed free of interest. 'These are debentures for seats in the Mound Stand and the Grand Stand. Seatholders lend the club money in return for the right to buy a ticket for that seat for a fixed period. Then they can ask for it back or leave it with us, and they're not all going to ask for their money back at the same time.'

Interest is paid on £2.8m, borrowed from NatWest and Barclays for the Media Centre and the Compton and Edrich stands. 'We've repaid what we're due to repay. We could pay it all off immediately. But we'd have to pay a penalty, so it's not worthwhile.'

The role of the finance committee, he says, is to give MCC the luxury of choice: 'A strong financial unit with good resources gives you the choice to make decisions. It's rather nice. We've done the Pavilion and we didn't go into overdraft on that job. We can finance it out of cash flow over two or three years. We can pay for MCC universities, and replace the roof of the Mound Stand.' Apparently, there are no immediate plans to replace the unglamorous Warner or Tavern Stands. Economics is more influential than aesthetics: the principal case for replacing existing buildings is to have new ones that increase capacity and income.

A banker's view of the balance sheet? 'Wearing my corporate hat, I'd say we were under-geared. I'd say either get on and develop the business, or return some capital to the shareholders,' says Stocken. In fact, the Estates Committee had come up with a proposal to increase revenue, in conjunction with a developer, by building houses, shops and possibly an hotel on land owned by Lord's. Stocken reports: 'The committee's reaction was "Hang on, this is not what we're about." '

Stocken himself is in no doubt about what MCC is about. The principal responsibility is to the ground. 'Lord's is the premier cricket ground in the world and we'd never give that up. It has to be in the best state to play cricket and we have to use the asset in the best way possible.' Next in the hierarchy of responsibility is MCC cricket – the 450 out-matches and the international tours. 'I put members third. They are not as important as the ground. One's a member on average for 35 years. We are itinerant. The ground is not itinerant.'

Stocken's is the voice of a beneficiary of this nation's remarkable prosperity in the past decade. To members who complain about the price of a cup of tea or a pint of beer he says: 'They just haven't got it in perspective any more. They forget that the subs at MCC are still incredibly low. What's their membership at the golf club? £1,000? MCC subscription is half a day's shooting.'

These views are heavily influenced by consumer surveys that show the importance of Lord's as a brand. 'The MCC brand may have great value for members, but it doesn't mean much to the outside world. It stands for the wrong things – establishment, won't change, fuddy-duddy, privileged, exclusive. What we're about is Lord's. People don't go to MCC, they go to Lord's. Frankly we need to downplay to the public the MCC brand.'

This is the new radicalism at MCC. Presumably Tom Graveney is a symbol of it. The hard-headed Oliver Stocken says: 'Here is a serious cricketer whom we all admired. He's not a President who wants to change the club, but he's got a fantastic touch. He's done it very well.'

WHO RUNS LORD'S?

The Committee Room at Lord's, which is approached through two sets of doors off the Long Room, is an inner sanctum. Plain members may glimpse members of the committee through a large central window as they sit watching play from their high chairs, but entrance is by invitation only. This is where MCC is governed. Although twelve of the members of the MCC Committee are elected by the whole membership, MCC is by no stretch of the imagination a democratic institution. In common with most London clubs, the Committee's proceedings are confidential, and meetings are not open to ordinary members, though half-yearly meetings are arranged at which members can question the Chairman. There is a faint air of mystery about the room.

A three-sided table made from wide wooden planks is set out for meetings of the MCC Committee and its various subsidiary committees, with a blotter and a list of the summer's fixtures at Lord's in front of each seat. A portrait of Thomas Lord hangs above the grey marble fireplace. Charles Fry sits in the long shadow of his grandfather, C. B. Fry. More recent worthies are the subjects of good watercolours by John Ward. The floor is carpeted, and a chandelier hangs from the decorated-plaster ceiling. It would be hard to sit there without being conscious of the ghosts of famous men who ran the game of cricket, and of the tradition they represent.

That does not mean things stay the same. In the first years of the twenty-first century, the power structure at MCC was reformed, and one of the

IN THE COMMITTEE ROOM: *'Friday 22nd July 2005 – I'm back in the Pavilion today, after yesterday's exciting play, and unlike yesterday where I was down at pitchside, today I am slightly removed from the action, sitting quietly in the corner of the Committee Room allowing the various committee members to enjoy (or rather commiserate as England decides to fall for 155 and let Australia back into bat again) the play through the fabulously large picture window. Very civilized with Tim serving tea and biscuits and then a little later Pimm's and champagne to fortify against Australia's strengthening lead…'*

consequences of these changes was to open up the Presidency to people like Tom Graveney, who had not been thrown up by the internal politics of the place. The last years of the old century had been turbulent. Like Britain in the 1960s, MCC had lost an empire and not yet found a role. Management had been dogged by cash problems associated with ambitious new buildings.

A working party in 1999 began looking at the balance between MCC's

private and public roles – as a private members' club and as the proprietors of England's leading Test ground. The Chairman was Sir Michael Jenkins, the former diplomat and EU civil servant, who had retired early to move into the City, where he joined the merchant bankers Kleinwort Benson as an executive director. Jenkins eventually headed the London office of Boeing, the American plane-makers. He had been an analyst, an adventurer and a lobbyist – all excellent qualifications for an inquiry chairman.

'There was a general feeling that there was a certain lack of management grip,' says Jenkins. Interdepartmental rivalry meant the finance and marketing departments were not speaking to each other. The absence of a club solicitor cost MCC up to £250,000 a year for outside legal advice. The division of power and responsibility between full-time management and

MCC members on committees was not clearly defined. Lord's had become a business with a turnover of more than £10m, but the relationship between cricket and commerce was uncharted and uncertain. MCC was full of lawyers and civil servants who didn't regard business as a thing to be encouraged. Jenkins recalls: 'We felt there were not enough people with business savvy.'

Jenkins sought out people such as Oliver Stocken and Charles Fry to join his working party, and co-opted Roger Knight. Initially, they contemplated a separation of the powers, running cricket and commerce independent of each other, but the idea did not flourish. MCC, they concluded, should remain a hybrid, governed by the members and run by the management, but their roles should be more clearly defined. Roger Knight, who had been a victim of the confusion, was entitled not to be second-guessed by the MCC Committee about matters that should have been his business.

The executive board was the new idea in Jenkins's report. The board would meet monthly, and take the day-to-day decisions on issues that need not detain the MCC Committee, which would concentrate on the big topics – senior appointments, serious cricket issues and the budget. There would then, Jenkins thought, be no reason why the MCC Committee need meet more than four times a year.

The report, titled 'Preparing for the Future', proposed that the traditional power base occupied by the Treasurer should no longer exist, and a club chairman should be appointed in his place. The Chairman would run meetings of both the Executive Board and the MCC Committee. The Secretary would get the additional title of Chief Executive. A deputy chief executive would be employed to run the commercial activities at Lord's. The President, whose term had earlier been lengthened to two years to let him find his feet under the Committee Room table, was to revert to a one-year term. The plan was that he 'should focus on representational duties as the titular head of MCC'.

Roger Knight saw the implications most clearly. 'It changed the way I have to work. When I first came in I felt like a bit of a headmaster. It was my ship and I ran it. After all, I had been a headmaster. The governing body met every two months, and I reported to them. I didn't have one specific boss. Now I report to the Chairman. I'm very conscious that I'm more accountable to one person and the Executive Board. They may not all be thinking the same. I suppose I've had to become more diplomatic and tactful.'

Some members of the committee felt it was being downgraded, and the suggestion that it ought to meet less regularly was rejected, but the principal proposals were adopted. As a reward for his labour, Jenkins became the first Chairman. He was succeeded in 1993 by Lord Alexander, who had been President after Tony Lewis. A successful barrister, who had represented Kerry Packer in the crucial case against MCC at the time of Packer's World Series Cricket, he had become chairman of NatWest bank, and guided much sponsorship money towards Lord's. On retirement from the bank, he became chairman of the Royal Shakespeare Company. As a classic poacher turned gamekeeper, he also moved to the top of the hierarchy at MCC, first as President and then as Chairman. (He was particularly gratified by the appointment of an in-house lawyer.) Bob Alexander was an enterprising figure, conciliatory at annual meetings, a keen moderniser and a good host. Sadly, he was disabled by a stroke near the end of his term, and Charles Fry took over the Chairmanship. Following Alexander, the new-style Presidents had been Ted Dexter, who pressed for MCC to become more involved in recreational cricket; the librettist Sir Tim Rice and Charles Fry, before he chose Tom Graveney in 2004.

MCC committee meetings remain confidential, but to lend bulk and balance to my inquiries at Lord's, I was invited to attend meetings of the MCC Committee, the Executive Board and the Membership Committee. I came away with a snapshot of the way MCC works now.

At the MCC Committee, Tom Graveney was flanked by Charles Fry and Oliver Stocken, who had assumed the title of Treasurer. Roger Knight sat beside Fry and on his left was Stephanie Lawrence, one of MCC's most able and experienced administrators, who took the minutes. Among the 22 members there was a decent representation of people who knew the game intimately. Besides Graveney, who had captained England for one match in 1968, the best-known face was Mike Gatting, then the last England captain to win the Ashes; Tony Lewis had also captained England. Colin Ingleby-Mackenzie and John Barclay were county captains at Hampshire and Sussex. Michael Sturt had kept wicket for Middlesex and Tim O'Gorman had spent years with Derbyshire. The fourth England captain in attendance was Rachael Heyhoe Flint, the first woman to be elected to the MCC Committee. Among the officials John Stephenson had captained Hampshire, and Knight himself is a former captain of Surrey.

Since the Pavilion was then a building site, the meeting took place in the restaurant in the Warner Stand. It was early in December and the pressing issue was the talks then taking place about TV rights for three years starting in 2006. The *Daily Telegraph* had been campaigning against the idea of an exclusive deal with Sky TV, which would remove Test cricket from all terrestrial TV. Anthony Wreford, chairman of the marketing committee, had already told the Chairman he thought it would be wrong for MCC to endorse such a deal. A move to Sky would have serious implications, not least for a generation of youngsters who would be prevented from watching Test cricket on TV if they did not have access to Sky. Wreford declared that it was MCC's responsibility as 'guardians of the game' to draw attention to this.

A committee member said that he believed the objective of the ECB's chief negotiator – Somerset's chairman Giles Clark – was to maximise TV revenue. Graveney confirmed this: earlier in the week he had met Clark at a funeral and Clark had told him: 'We need the money. We can't do without it.' To sugar the pill, Clark added they were trying to bring forward the Test highlights programme on TV into the early evening, away from the ghetto it occupied around midnight. The MCC Committee was not appeased.

Since an exclusive deal with Sky would reduce the size of the TV audience for cricket, revenue from perimeter advertising would fall, but by how much? And what could they do about it? Trying to unite with other Test grounds would be a start. But was it still possible to influence the decision, which was due imminently? Roger Knight had some of the answers. He sits as MCC's representative on the ECB management committee and is a Director of ECB. He felt that there was no viable alternative to Sky's bid – the only other option would have left the ECB lacking in the necessary funds to service and provide for the game in England and Wales.

The truth was that the MCC's Committee was incapable of influencing the decision. Realising this encouraged a subversive idea: Why not leave the ECB? When the ECB insisted that England's embarrassing tour of Zimbabwe should go ahead, members of the MCC Committee had raised the issue. The Sky deal might revive it.

The MCC Committee was also powerless to stop the ICC quitting its office behind the Compton Stand. For decades MCC was the ICC, and after the ICC had finally declared its independence, the offices stayed at Lord's. But it had had a better offer from Dubai, and was determined to leave London completely for brand new offices in the Gulf. One problem had been the Treasury's refusal to grant tax exemption to international sports federations located in London. Shouldn't MCC write to the Treasury? Or was it a bit late? The committee felt it probably was too late, but it was worth doing anyway.

The long agenda dealt with a range of subjects, some substantial, some less so. The Laws of Cricket working party was concerned with new ICC regulations about chucking (the term used to describe illegal bowling actions), and by the bonded graphite strip on Kookaburra bats used by (among others) Australia's captain Ricky Ponting and England's Graham Thorpe. 'This is the thin end of a very thick wedge,' declared one member. Next: there would be some sort of celebration of the life of Keith Miller during the Ashes Test. Next: the commercial imperative for the first Test against Bangladesh would be to fill the ground rather than to maximise income. This meant free admission for thousands of schoolchildren.

Next: MCC had been willing to spend £400,000 at auction to buy an L. S. Lowry painting of a cricket match, but had been seriously outbid (the painting went for £700,000). Next: the International Olympic Committee would be visiting Lord's in February and May to judge its fitness to hold the archery competition in 2012 if London won its Olympic bid. The last act was a long debate about debenture holders. It was complicated, and, despite its having been raised before, and a wealth of written documentation, the Chairman in charge felt some members were still not concentrating. That was it. Members who did not have to dash (for it was late) milled round the bar for a glass of wine, which they deserved.

At a meeting of the Membership Committee in mid-May, MCC got down to the nitty-gritty of running a cricket club at Lord's. Some subjects on the agenda seemed insignificant, but exuded underlying significance.

Item: the Bradman portrait. The curator of the Museum and of the paintings, Adam Chadwick, had hung this just outside the Long Room bar, facing a lift, perhaps because the portrait makes no reference to cricket. The committee was told that the Aussies wouldn't like it. Robin Marlar, present as President-designate, said the best place for that portrait was the basement. The decision was to leave the decision to the curator.

Item: a member had asked whether it would be permissible for members to remove their jackets in the Pavilion for the carnival atmosphere of Middlesex's Twenty20 game against Surrey in 2005. The committee member who thought this was worth considering was in a minority of one. The secretariat pointed out that people had already been told what to wear. That was a jacket and tie. Furthermore, since there was a cooling system, the Pavilion was comfortable even in the hottest weather. The conclusion was that some formalities needed to be retained. Not to do so would be the thin end of another wedge.

Item: the committee was concerned about standards of behaviour over scarce seats for the Ashes Test. Action was needed to prevent members bagging more than one seat when they arrived early in the morning: to do so was 'bad form and not clubbable'. But not as bad as selling tickets at black-market prices on eBay or through the newspapers: twelve black-market tickets had already turned up, and some of the culprits identified. Punishments were proposed. Members caught selling their tickets ought to be suspended for one or two years, and prevented from buying any tickets until after the next Ashes series in 2009.

Item: the price of a cup of tea and a pint of beer, a subject of scandal and concern among a vocal minority. Tea, which had cost 80p now cost members £1.30, the same as the general public pays. Beer had risen to £3 a pint, with a 20p discount for members at their bars. One defence of the price rises was that members had been told that some higher prices would be a consequence of in-house catering. This line was unlikely to appease disgruntled pensioners. The committee was conscious of the danger that catering profits might rise substantially, and that MCC would stand accused of 'extravagance, greed, and extortion'. One member commented plaintively: 'Surely this committee ought to have some say.'

Like busy managers in a public company, the Executive Board meets early, at 8.30 in the morning, and it starts on the dot. On a table there are the makings of a continental breakfast, coffee and croissants, orange juice and fresh fruit. Whether it was intended or not, executives are outnumbered by non-executives by six to four. 'I'm not sure that it's the right term to call it the executive board,' says Roger Knight – but it is the only board the executive managers have got.

Latest sales figures are provided for the Bangladesh Test and the special one-day game to be played on 14 June to raise funds for the Tsunami victims – sales good but not spectacular. Good news was that an overseas broadcaster had paid US$250,000 for TV rights. Sad news was that Sachin Tendulkar would not be fit, though he would be present, maybe to assist Shane Warne who had agreed to bowl an over in the middle at the highest bidder at auction. Shirts and sweaters worn by the stars would also be auctioned. Given MCC's distaste for unauthorised sales on the net, management wondered whether they would be right use to eBay. It would.

MCC's Head of Cricket suggested that an experimental orange cricket ball should be used in the Tsunami game. 'How much does it swing,' said one member, who did not want players like Brian Lara and Rahul Dravid getting out too cheaply to freak swing.

Bagging seats at the Ashes Test was raised once more, and it was agreed that members of the membership committee would be on hand to remind recalcitrant members of the rule against bagging more than one seat, and to help stewards apply it. Board members learned that the Australian team had declined an invitation to the touring team dinner, but it was hoped that they would still attend the customary MCC reception on day two of the Test, and a dinner would be held the following day for retired Australian players who had made the trip.

The chairman of the Cricket Committee reported on the experiment with drop-in pitches. They had been used for nets the previous week and he reported that they were much better than he had thought they would be: two had played extremely well. The third had cracked badly. But the principle seemed to be quite sound. This sounded like a go ahead, though the Cricket Committee did not intend to replace any of the major match pitches in the middle of the square. Pitches would be dropped in towards the Tavern Stand and used for non first-class matches. The cost would be substantial – £100,000 for the pitch transporter, for a start. The Cricket Committee was asked to produce facts and figures.

The board learned of a strange problem in the Pavilion. The players' habit of dragging their cricket bags, or 'coffins', down the stairs was damaging the staircase. What was to be done?

'We could ask them to carry them down.'

'No, Chairman. I don't think we could.'

'Could we employ someone to carry them?'

The reply was unspoken: Up to a point, Mr Chairman.

The last major item was the 'Chance to Shine' campaign, which intends to raise large sums of money to get cricket back into state schools. Leaders of the campaign had asked MCC to join them and their response had been guarded. They were not unsupportive in principle, but they wanted to know how the money would be spent and who would be spending it. MCC already spends £1.3m a year on recreational cricket, though as the Head of Cricket reminded them, it was still poor on state schools cricket.

The conversation meandered along familiar channels, until Tom Graveney put in his two pennyworth: 'This has gone on at practically every meeting, and we've always said the same thing.'

Despite efforts by Sir Michael Jenkins to streamline and rationalise decision-making in MCC committees, repetition was systemic. Instead of streamlining the administration, the Executive Board seemed only to have added an additional layer of it. Of course, members of a club do not demand the same organisational efficiency as shareholders in profit-making companies. Efficiency is a good idea, but, if it is hard to come by, how much does it matter? MCC's healthy balance sheet suggests that the management is doing something right. And as long as committee members are happy to spend the time they do on such a wide range of topics, the Jenkins revolution might remain half-baked.

PLAYING REAL TENNIS

———

Most MCC members do not notice the real tennis court in the dull, brick building behind the Pavilion – unless they patronise the champagne bar that opens during Test matches. This is sited in the room where spectators watch real tennis, sitting behind a rectangular hole in the wall known as the dedans. But there is an active playing membership of two hundred, and in 2005 they had the added excitement of the European Open Singles Championship. Also present was the real tennis world champion, an Australian called Robert Fahy, and a keen, but rather less accomplished player, Prince Edward, Earl of Wessex.

The title 'European Open' is a bit of swagger, because in Europe the game is played only in Britain and France. There are courts in the United States and Australia too, but that is all. Real tennis was originally a French game, known as palm play, or *jeu de paume* and the once-celebrated art gallery that stands on the Place de la Concorde was formerly a tennis court. There were about six hundred such courts in France until the Revolution, when tennis was denounced as a relic of a decadent aristocracy; most courts then became theatres, so not all was lost. The name was 'palm play' because the ball was hit with the hand, sometimes gloved, sometimes not. The problem of wear and tear on the hand was eventually addressed by substituting a small racquet in the shape of a hand, and that is how real tennis racquets still differ from the more regular oval shapes used for squash and lawn tennis.

There were only a few vacant seats at the start of the European Open on a fine day, late in spring. 'Full' indicates 30 or so spectators, mostly men, in three rows of seats behind the dedans at the server's end of the court, and a further 20 or so at the side of the court. The dedans is covered with thick netting, since one object of the game is score points by hitting the ball into the hole. Spectators mingle with players at the back of the room. There is a smart new electronic scoreboard on the side wall.

Tennis has been played at Lord's since 1839. The court was the third building to be erected on the ground, after the Pavilion and the Tavern. Until lawn tennis became fashionable towards the end of the nineteenth century – the laws were originally written in 1876, by MCC – there was no need to call it 'real', but that had been added by the time the old court was demolished to make way for the Mound Stand. The new tennis and squash courts were opened on 1 January 1900, on a site in the capacious back garden of number three Grove End Road, which backed on to the Pavilion. They are still there, alongside the Museum, and busy enough for the real tennis players to be on the lookout for a site for a second real tennis court.

Brian Sharp, an experienced hand on the court at Lord's, was my tutor. Looking through the dedans, he pointed to the low roof along two sides of the court, known as the penthouse roof, with a buttress – called the tambour – and a grille on the far wall. Hit the grille and it's a winner, like the dedans. Modern players can only speculate about the origins of these curious specifications. One theory is that they come from a thirteenth century medieval marketplace: stalls under the roof, with the buttress belonging to an invisible church. Similar surroundings could be found in medieval monasteries or castles, and another theory is that the game was invented by monks with time on their hands and energy to burn.

As the game developed, racquets that could impart cut and spin on the ball became common, and covered courts were built so that rain could not stop play. That was when it became the favourite game of the royal court. Real tennis was played by some of Prince Edward's distant ancestors. Henry VII passed on a love of the game – and a fondness for gambling on the result

– to his son Henry VIII, who built courts at Hampton Court – still in use – and in Whitehall. The foundations of that were recently rediscovered under the Cabinet Office.

The scoring system, French in origin, is familiar because it was adopted by lawn tennis players, but the rules are not so simple. When the umpire says 'Chase, second gallery', one of the players is being told exactly where in the court he must hit the ball to win a point. It is a subtle game of angles as the ball, which is heavier than a tennis ball, bounces off the penthouse roof and the buttress, but it can be played at a gentle pace that allows skilful players to carry on into their sixties.

The professional players who turned up for the European Championships do not play at a gentle pace. Athleticism, speed and skill are all

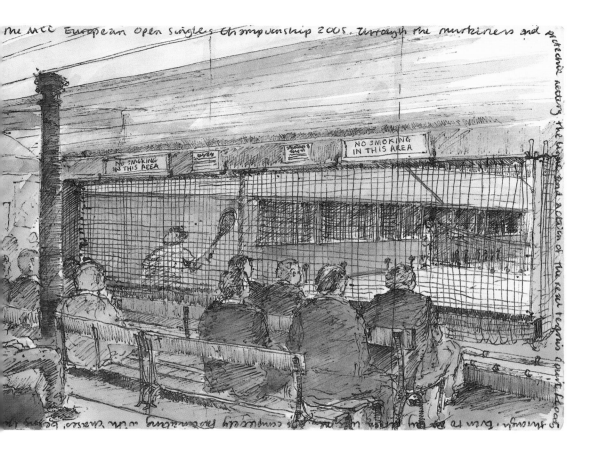

REAL TENNIS: *'Friday 20th May 2005 – Through reception and into the murky 'dedans'*
to get your seat for the European Open Singles Championship 2005. Through the murkiness
and protective netting, the light and action of the real tennis court floods through. Even to a
lay person like me, it's completely fascinating with 'chases' being laid and lost, lots of galleries
and hazards to take into account, and as the marker keeps saying, 'better than' and 'worse
than' – it's all gripping stuff…'

required. It is soon clear that the best players can command the middle of
the court, directing their own shots along the side wall, off the back wall and
into the corners, so that the return, if there is one, comes back to them in
the middle of the court. You don't need an intimate acquaintance with the
rules to enjoy watching the best players perform.

The best of all is Robert Fahy, a name which suggests distant ancestry in the west of Ireland. A great-great-great grandfather had emigrated to Tasmania, and Fahy went to university in Hobart where there is a real tennis court. He was so promising as a student that he was taken on as assistant professional when he graduated. He won his first Australian Open championship in 1993, and by the turn of the century he was ranked number one in the world. He has since won the UK professional singles title four years in a row, and the American version in three of the past four years. Sharp says Fahy's special quality is aggression, though there is no evidence of it as he chats while he watches an early round in the championship. He is slim, with hair greying prematurely for a man aged 37. His manner is open and informative. In the small world of real tennis, everyone knows everyone else, and he mixes easily with the spectators. Indeed, he might have played some of them, because a generous handicapping system enables old goats to compete with champions.

I asked him what other game has most in common with real tennis, expecting him to say squash or Eton fives, which is played with a gloved hand in courts with a buttress and a step on the floor. 'Cricket', replied Fahy. Really? 'It's a heavy ball with low bounce. You have to watch the spin, and cut of the ball, and you play side-on.' The comparison was not immediately obvious, but, as if to clinch his case, he added: 'It's a front-foot game.'

Tom Graveney watched Fahy playing in the Championship final – which he won – a few days later and was struck by his ability to play balls that bounced unpredictably from the buttress. He also took note of Fahy's fitness. Old cricketers are not easily impressed by the fitness of modern athletes – their fitness regime was to play six days a week and drink six pints at the end of each of them. But he also understood why real tennis players need to be fit: 'They don't sit down between games. There are no official breaks. It's a continuous match.'

Players and members wore evening dress at a dinner in the Long Room at the end of the championships. Prince Edward was guest of honour. Royal guests sometimes like to see the texts of speeches that will be made on occasions like this, and Colin Maynard, the assistant secretary, dutifully sent a version of the Graveney speech to the Prince's private secretary. Graveney, thinking it was a bit formal, added a couple of favourite stories from his extensive repertoire.

He recalled the first time he met Prince Edward's mother. Len Hutton was England's captain, and when he and the Queen reached Graveney, Hutton forgot Graveney's name. On another occasion, when Hutton was introducing the team to the Archbishop of Canterbury, he was presented as 'Tom Goddard'. 'I don't think I made a hit with Len, somehow or other,' he says.

But the subject of his favourite royal story was the Prince's father. A game was being played at Arundel to raise money for the National Playing Fields Association, a favourite charity of the Duke of Edinburgh. The Duke of Norfolk asked Graveney to join his team. 'It was a lovely bunch of people,' says Graveney, remembering Doug Wright, Willy Watson and George Tribe – three fine players of his generation, now all dead. 'I'd got about 14 or 15 when the Duke of Edinburgh came on to bowl. He was a big chap, he knew what he was up to, and he spun it. I went to sweep it and got a top edge. It went up in the air and this bloke ran round and caught it. I was out, caught Wing-Commander Chinnery, bowled the Duke of Edinburgh. You can't be out better than that.'

Had he given his wicket away?

'Definitely not,' he says. 'But I did get the OBE in the next honours list.'

A TEST DEBUT FOR BANGLADESH

A number of Bangladesh's cricketers had seen Lord's when they were invited to a reception in the museum in the autumn of 2004, to familiarise them with the ground before their first Test in England. But they needed more experience than that to quell their nerves before their first Test at Lord's. By the time they arrived in England in May, they had lost 31 of the 36 Tests they had played since the ICC prematurely voted them into the top division in 2000. Four had been drawn; the solitary win was against Zimbabwe in January 2005.

Never mind. Selling the tickets had been a challenge and Simon Wakefield's department had performed manfully. The ambitious attempt to sell tickets to the Bangladeshi community in the East End through the Sonali bank had raised a meagre £2,000; but MCC had done as it intended, and shown it was doing its best for the Test minnows.

Lord's shifted into operational mode on the Monday of the week of the Test. Thousands of linen tablecloths and napkins arrived from the hirers. The cost of fresh linen: £10,000. A fresh delivery would arrive each day during the Test. Juggernauts carrying beer from the Courage Brewery in Greenford would arrive on Wednesday. The new concessions in the Food Village behind the Edrich Stand were taking up their positions. Umbrellas, tables and chairs were being set up by Green's of Mayfair's Seafood and Champagne Bar in the Harris Garden. On Wednesday, the less experienced half of the 600 casual catering staff would arrive to be taught, if they did not already know, how to pour a gin and tonic and a pint of beer. When the stores had been deposited in the boxes, the carpets had a final hoovering.

MCC followed routine for the run-up to a Test. On Monday, a dinner was held in the Committee Dining Room for the Bangladesh team and officials; a reception would be held for both teams in the Committee Room at the end of the second day's play. Since they were not due back until 2010 or 2011, it would, for some of the team, be the first and last time they would play at Lord's. Both Tom Graveney and Charles Fry gave them the same message at the Monday dinner: make the most of the experience, and enjoy it. They were clearly enjoying the dinner. Linda Le Ker, the chef in the committee and players' dining rooms, assuming that most of the team were vegetarians, had prepared a special dish for the Bangladeshis. But they preferred her chicken and meat. The vegetarian lasagne all came back, except one helping – eaten with gusto by Colin Ingleby-Mackenzie, one of MCC's trustees.

One Bangladesh player who would almost certainly be back was the tiny figure of Mushfiqur Rahim, who was to make his Test debut, still aged sixteen, the youngest member of a team whose average was surely the lowest in the history of Test cricket. He boasted to Graveney that he had already scored two first-class hundreds. 'You've only got 120 to go before you catch up with me,' replied Graveney.

The weather on the first morning of the Test was uninviting: low cloud cover and a suggestion of rain in the air. Michael Vaughan won the toss, and did Bangladesh no favour by sending them in to bat. The new ball jagged and swung sharply, but Javed Omar and Nafees Iqbal survived for 45 minutes or so. Neither Matthew Hoggard nor Stephen Harmison had taken advantage of conditions that were wholly foreign to the Bangladesh batsmen, but when Iqbal edged Harmison to Marcus Trescothick in the slips with the score on 31, the bowlers' length and line reappeared, and Bangladesh's humiliation began. Five wickets fell before lunch, and they were all out for 108 in 38.2 overs.

By the time England's first wicket fell, the sun was out, batting conditions were fine, and they already had a lead of 40. England's second wicket

Friday May 27th 2005 It's day two of England v Bangladesh and the sun has come out a... sketch "in progress"...

did not fall until after lunch the next day, when the total was 403 and both Trescothick and Vaughan had scored hundreds. Friday was a beautiful day for cricket, the hottest of the year so far, but the mood in the President's Box was not happy. The fear was that England would declare when they had a lead of around 300 and try to win in two days. With so many boxes sold and so much food and drink ordered, no play on the third day would be very bad news.

Graveney slipped into the ECB box and asked the senior men present whether the two sides couldn't play a 20-overs-a-side game if the Test was over on the third day. 'They said, "Not a chance". I don't know about modern cricketers.' He remembered playing without complaint in a 30-over exhibition match against New Zealand in 1958 when a Test finished early.

THE CAMERAMEN AT PITCH LEVEL: '*Friday May 27th 2005 – it's day two of England v. Bangladesh and the sun has come out, and well, it's warm and wonderful, so I've climbed down from the Media Podium Pod and down to where it all happens at pitch side – watching the cameras watching the cricket. My cunning plan was uncovered though, as I turned around to find a Channel 4 camera trained on my sketchbook – I guess as one of those little distraction pieces – not quite as exciting as a pitch invasion, but hey the back of my head and this sketch in progress now have their few minutes of fame…*'

But Vaughan did not declare as soon as he might have done, allowing Ian Bell and Graham Thorpe to spend time at the crease before declaring shortly after tea, at 528 for 3. By the close on the second day, Bangladesh had reduced the arrears from 420 to 330, but had already lost five wickets, including their captain and best batsman, Habibul Bashar, who had been dismissed hooking for 3 in the first innings and was out the same way for only 16 in the second.

Opinions about Bangladesh's performance in the Media Centre and among English sections of the crowd were both sympathetic and contemptuous. But when I sat with Graveney and made a couple of jokes, suggesting that MCC Young Cricketers could have given them a game, or that maybe we should revert to Victorian style and have England play XXII of Bangladesh, he refused to make fun of them. 'It won't help their cricket,' he said. 'They've got so many people who want to play, they need encouragement. They will be good one day.'

But he had no illusions about here and now. 'I want to hide my eyes at some of the shots they've played. One problem is that they haven't learned how to duck.' Poor Mushfiqur Rahim had tried to fend off a fierce bouncer from an uncompromising Andrew Flintoff, and, for his pains, was caught off an edge by the 'keeper.

That evening both teams were in the Committee Room. Had any England players asked Graveney's advice? 'They didn't ask me and I wouldn't presume.' But he had been interested in Vaughan's innings, which had been scratchy until he settled down after an hour or so on Friday morning. 'He's not a good starter,' said Graveney. Watching him play in Australia in the winter of 2002/03 had been a revelation: 'Whether it was a good idea to move him out of the opening spot, I don't know, but in Australia he took the Aussies on.' Graveney had especially admired the short-arm pull to the square-leg boundary: 'Very effective.' High praise.

Public address announcements on Friday afternoon told ticket holders for the third day's play that they would get a full refund if fewer than ten overs were bowled, and half their money back if fewer than twenty-five overs were needed to finish the game. Refunds are covered by an ECB insurance policy, but MCC still stood to lose on catering if few spectators turned up on Saturday.

Saturday morning was sunny, and a surprising number of ticket holders did show, about 10,000 of them. After ten minutes they must have thought in terms of brunch not lunch. Before Bangladesh had reached 100, three more wickets had fallen, but a gutsy innings by the 'keeper Khaled Mashud batting at number seven, in a ninth wicket stand of 62 with Anwar Hossain, stretched the innings out to 39.5 overs. This was just enough to provide the spectators with a reason for turning up, but not enough to prevent them getting half their money back. Graveney's special day in the President's Box began on time and ended long after England had won by an innings and 261 runs. He had invited old pals and former professionals from Worcestershire. Arthur Milton of Gloucestershire – the last man to be capped by England at cricket and football – joined them. But the family party he had planned to hold in his box on the Sunday had to be cancelled.

After the game, Habibul Bashar had little to say in English, but when he was asked in Bengali how he felt, he said that Bangladesh had come to Lord's hoping to play well enough to take away happy memories. 'But we didn't do anything well. I'm really unhappy with myself. It is the worst disappointment.' Here was one cricketer who had not been able to take Graveney's advice and enjoy his first game at Lord's. The sense of let-down was palpable.

The game had been watched by 59,100 spectators, 10,000 fewer than the ticket office had hoped, though receipts – of £1,137,000 – were better than budgeted for. But a Test won in fewer than seven sessions is too perfunctory to satisfy either players – though the winners are glad of a couple of extra days off – or spectators. But MCC did have one item to put in its compliments file. The lofty figure of Scyld Berry, the *Sunday Telegraph*'s experienced and exacting cricket correspondent, had this to say on the Sunday after the Test was over: 'MCC had a good game. In 1984 MCC did their best to deter spectators from Sri Lanka's inaugural Test, and deserved to be called the most backward-looking cricket club in the world, but now they are the most progressive. Free tickets for 5,000 schoolchildren in the May-time Test, innovative architecture, and stewards saying "goodnight" as you leave the ground are only a start. MCC was just about the only friend Bangladesh had before the Asian powers wanted their vote, and sent tours

THE CORONATION GARDEN: *'Saturday 23rd July 2005 – The Ashes Series is not the only competition going on at Lord's today – there is also one going on for the perfect picnic pitch here in the Coronation Gardens. As play started W.G. Grace, a blackbird and myself peacefully shared the garden, but as lunchtime drew near, crowds swelled and not a blade of grass to be seen. Hence Mr Grace is about twice the size he should be as he ably defends his corner, but then in the minds of all cricket fans W.G. Grace's stature is that great anyway… So that's all fine then…'*

there. As the Bangladeshis went out to bat here, the steward at the Pavilion probably said "goodnight" to them too.'

One rewarding task had to be performed while the wickets were falling. The Test was the first opportunity to taste-test the food at Lord's, which was provided by its own kitchens and by the new concessions. To lend authority

to my opinion, I asked a proper gourmet to provide a critical guide. Matthew Fort writes for the *Guardian*, and was recovering from having just been declared Food Writer of the Year and author of the Food Book of the Year. As an MCC member, Fort was also keen to watch some cricket.

We started with a glass of champagne in Green's of Mayfair's Seafood and Champagne Bar in the Harris Garden, sipping while sitting comfortably in front of a large flat TV screen relaying the action in the middle. The cost? £17 for two plastic flutes of Veuve Cliquot: 'a decent champagne very well chilled,' said Fort. The wine went to the bottom of the stem of the glasses. 'Elegant', he added.

Behind the Tavern Stand, Fort inspected the menu at the heavily refurbished Tavern Bar. 'Caesar Salad and Salad Niçoise for your figure-conscious eater. Steak and Kidney Pie for the more traditional eater, middle-aged and above. Well judged,' was the verdict.

When we reached the Food Village, Fort made straight for Helen Browning's Organic Flying Pig. Browning, it appears, is the queen of the organic food movement, producing meat at her farm in Wiltshire, where she conducts a thriving mail-order business. We ordered bacon rolls. 'Good bacon, good porky flavour with a nice layer of fat.' Price: £5.50, or £8 for a steak sandwich. The counter-man recognised Matthew Fort, but I declare that flattery did not affect his judgement. The bacon roll tasted so good that I went for another the following morning, and was deterred only by the length of the queue.

Fort approved of the Real Cornish Pasty Co., where an authentic pasty can be had for £3.50, and the Sea Shell of Lisson Grove, a reputable local fish-and-chip shop selling cod and chips for £7.95. The Prime Burger Co. was advertising 100 per cent Scottish Angus beefburgers: cost £5. But Matthew had moved on to Imli@Lord's, a curry house inspired by Tamarind, an Indian restaurant in the West End that has one Michelin star. His vegetarian samosa was a bit too greasy, he said, but still fair. The tandoori chicken salad with Tamarind sauce did better: 'Spicy chicken, and not in the least dried out.' Prices from £3.50 to £6.

Back at the champagne bar we bought Pimm's to slake our thirst – two half pints, £9 in all. At Carte d'Or ice cream, which is made by Walls, he declared his preference for an ordinary Walls ice cream. I liked my vanilla cone. Leaving the Food Village we paused to taste glasses of the Australian Wolf Blass's cabernet sauvignon and chardonnay. Wolf Blass is the official supplier of wine to all England's Test grounds – which is good news because both were judged decent house wines.

On our way back to the Pavilion we paused for an excellent espresso at Sagafreddo, the Italian coffee specialists. It may be the first decent cup of coffee to be served at Lord's in the present ground's 191-year history. While England were ruthlessly piling on runs in the middle, Fort was in the mood for a pint of bitter when we got back to the Pavilion, and chose Young's over

London Pride. This was accompanied by a steak roll, which we shared. The meat was delicious pink fillet, though Fort thought the small plastic sachets of horseradish 'a bit infra dig'. Price £6.50.

Not everyone was happy with the food. One member approached the trolley holding open his steak roll, asking 'Where's my salad?' Learning that salad was not included, he said: 'I thought this place was supposed to be getting better, not worse.' Never mind the quality, feel the width.

In the Tavern Stand, Fort summed up. It was good news, he said, that Lord's had dismissed for ever the smell of rancid onions and cheap hot dogs. 'Good food starts with good ingredients, and what they've tried to do is attract high-quality food producers. Helen Browning is an excellent statement of intent.'

We had heard murmurs about prices on the food stalls far higher than a hot dog with fried onions. But Fort refused to be perturbed. 'Of course it's more expensive than McDonald's. For a start, good food costs money, and also I'm assuming that everyone's got to make a profit out of this.' His concern was with quality, and virtually everything we tasted met with his approval.

By taking catering back in house, David Batts, MCC's commercial mind, had managed to change the image of Lord's. Watching a Lord's Test is not going to be like going to Edgbaston or Trent Bridge, and not at all like the dreary grounds at Old Trafford and Headingley. Food and drink at Lord's was now firmly established in another league. The management would be best-pleased if we thought 'Wimbledon': 'That's the model for Lord's,' says Iain Wilton, the Head of Communications. At the New Lord's, spectators were no longer expected to come just for the cricket, but to share the experience of a day at Lord's. Since 1991, Britain has become one of the world's most prosperous economies, and, like it or not, Lord's reflects the remarkable new wealth of the nation's capital.

REMEMBERING THE TSUNAMI

When the Tsunami struck on Boxing Day, killing as many as a quarter of a million people, the first priority was to feed and house the survivors. But as news of all the consequences of this terrible natural disaster became known, other casualties struck a chord. One of these was the cricket ground at Galle in south-west Sri Lanka, where Shane Warne had taken his 500th Test wicket. It stands on a peninsula in the shadow of a fine stone fort, with the sea washing in towards the cover and square-leg boundaries. Aerial pictures showed that it had been devastated.

Restoring the ground at Galle seemed like the perfect project for MCC. In the week after the disaster £25,000 was promised as a down payment, with more to follow from the proceeds of a one-day game between MCC and an International XI on 14 June. The £25,000 stayed in MCC bank, however, because no one in Sri Lanka could be found to account for the way the money was spent. Besides, sketchy information from Colombo suggested that influential figures did not want to redevelop Galle at all. The project went on hold.

MCC's intention was to parade a number of the world's greatest cricketers at the Tsunami game, though players from England and Australia would not be available (they were to play a Twenty20 match the night before). The response was gratifying. A team from MCC and an International XI would be captained by Brian Lara and Sachin Tendulkar, two of the finest batsmen in the history of cricket. Six Indians in the two squads guaranteed a sizeable Indian contingent at Lord's; South Africa contributed four players; West Indies three; and there were two New Zealanders, two Pakistanis, two Sri Lankans and one Zimbabwean. There was one Australian – but that was Shane Warne, who was not involved in Australia's one-day series in England.

Mick Hunt was asked to prepare a good batting wicket. John Stephenson's proposal that an experimental orange ball should be used was rejected because no one knew how much it would swing, and no one wanted wonderful stroke players to be victims of unpredictable movement. A piece of bad news was that Tendulkar needed surgery to his elbow, but he promised to be there. He said he would be happy to coach the punter who was willing to pay to face an over from Shane Warne during the lunch interval. The happy victim would be the highest bidder in an auction; the money would go to the appeal.

Ticket sales were promising. Tom Graveney sent a letter to members saying that, since they would not be paying to get in, a donation would be in order to the Leonard Cheshire Fund – which would distribute the money raised. (He did not put it quite that bluntly.) A week before the game, Roger Knight wrote another letter telling members that, since relatively few Rover tickets had been bought, MCC would sell members' seats in the Tavern Stand to the general public. This would not only raise money, it might also reduce the embarrassment caused on some big match days – one-day games especially – when empty seats in the Pavilion and the members' stands left gaping white spaces in contrast to the sea of faces in a sell-out crowd in the public stands.

Drama before match day: Chris Gayle's flight from Jamaica was cancelled, and he arrived at Heathrow less than four hours before play began. Poor bloke; he opened the batting for MCC and was lbw to Chaminda Vaas for four. There were 21,165 paying customers at £30, plus members – maybe 24,000 in all. Graveney was in the President's Box entertaining the players' wives and girlfriends, which he did not regard as a chore. He was struck by how much the Indian wives preferred gossip to cricket. But he was distracted in mid-morning by some bad news. The

THE TSUNAMI APPEAL MATCH: *'Tuesday 14th June 2005. What a world of difference a single word embodies in different contexts. Here today Mexican style 'waves' flow around the stands here and everyone here is in support for those affected by the terrible Tsunami 'waves'. Worlds apart indeed. Here in the near capacity crowds and also down on the pitch there are many different nationalities, cultures and religions all mingled together to watch Brian Lara lead the International XI against Mr Fleming and the MCC team for a stunning match, and all for a truly exceptional cause…'*

auction to find a bidder willing to pay to face an over from Shane Warne had gone sour. The winning bid on eBay was £50,000 but the address and phone number proved to be false. MCC had been hoaxed. Same with the second bid. What to do instead during the long lunch break?

Charles Fry suggested to Graveney that the President should put on his pads and take the over from Warne himself. He had not batted for three

today mexican style 'waves' flow around the stands and everyone here is in support for those affected by the terrible tsunami 'waves'. Worlds apart indeed

Here in the near capacity crowds and also down on the pitch there are many varied and different makeup

Karen Neale

years since he had a net at Malvern, aged 75, but that did not worry him. 'Picking up a bat is like riding a bike,' he says. Not Tendulkar's, however: 'it's too heavy'. He did not think he would be taking advice from the Little Master: 'Wouldn't need it. When you've reached a certain standard, you play that way.' Sadly for connoisseurs of bizarre confrontations at the wicket, Roger Knight needed to be sure that alternative lunchtime entertainment was in place before the Graveney/Warne scenario had emerged. The Christ's Hospital school big band would play in the interval. A delightful fantasy had turned out to be no more than that, though the story did enter Graveney's repertoire.

But the crowd had already seen Warne, who was not treated with much respect, conceding 64 runs off eight overs, taking two wickets only in the last over of the innings. Lara used ten bowlers, including himself (0 for 19 off two overs), and there were some easy runs to be had at the death; in 50 overs MCC scored 327 for 7. When he batted, Lara played two late cuts to the boundary so fast and so fine that if you hadn't seen them leave the bat, you might have called them byes. But Anil Kumble, Harbhajan Singh and Gayle, now restored, proved irresistible. For the record, MCC won by 112 runs.

Graveney hurried over from the box to present the players, who were clustered on the grass in front of the Pavilion, with their medals, and to thank Hunt for a perfect wicket, and the crowd for coming. He had a few words with each of the players, telling Lara that he was the best in the world. Graveney was struck by the solemn manner in which Sourav Ganguly removed his smart new MCC cap as he approached him. The biggest roar from the crowd was for Tendulkar as he got his medal. As Graveney and his MCC colleagues had a drink with the players, their wives and sweethearts in the Committee Room, it was the cheers for Tendulkar that lingered in his memory: 'They show Lord's is an international cricket ground. It's different from everywhere else.'

In the printing office behind the Museum, Amy Christie was inputting into her computer the last dismissals, the bowling figures and printing the completed scorecard. It was available at Amy's window 30 minutes after stumps were drawn. During the day, a visitor needs only to tap on the window to get the latest scorecard, price 50p. After each dismissal, a fax arrives on Amy's desk from the scorers' box. Towards the end of the International XI's innings, it was hard for her to keep up, but if a caller cared to wait for a minute or so, she would key in the latest dismissal to produce an up-to-the-minute card.

Lord's scorecards, measuring 9 and a half by 5 inches, are alleged to have been measured to fit a gentleman's jacket pocket, which might be why the sale of scorecards is falling. Outside the Pavilion, jackets are little worn at Lord's so there are fewer pockets to put scorecards in. In the old days, the printing office worked on the basis that three-quarters of the spectators would buy a scorecard; now it's closer to one-quarter of them.

Sales began to fall when the old printing office moved from the dingy passage under the old Grand Stand to its new location. That was when Lord's dispensed with the romance of the system of hand-set type that would have been familiar to William Caxton, and adopted new printing technology. Now only 4,000 to 5,000 cards are printed overnight before a big game.

After play starts, Amy's clients are 'anoraks mostly,' according to Andy Anderton, who runs the printing office. Anderton wears a gold stud in his ear, a fashion item normally worn at Lord's only in the dressing rooms by young professional cricketers, and his job runs in the family. His father worked in the old printing office until his retirement following the NatWest final in 1996. Anderton started work immediately after that.

Anderton had served his apprenticeship on the *Watford Observer* before going to work in the printing trade, where he learned to use the new, computer-led technology. He must also have absorbed some fond feelings for Lord's, but he did not tell his father that he was applying to be head printer, or the interviewers that he was his father's son. 'I wanted to get it on merit,' he says.

The office is crowded with machines. Beyond the high-spec graphic computers that drive desktop publishing, there are piles of different sizes of blank paper for mailings to members, menu cards, invitations, even pass-out tickets. The annual report is prepared in Anderton's office. Three of them work there, and Anderton is proud of the quality of their work and level of productivity (the old office was staffed by four, plus a part-timer). He thinks the in-house printing operation must save MCC as much as £100,000 a year – though he cannot be precise.

Not many anoraks waited outside Amy's window after the Tsunami game. A couple of weeks later, after the dramatic tie between England and Australia in the NatWest Series final, sales at the window were brisk, and hundreds more were snapped up at the North Gate by people wanting a souvenir of a wonderful game of cricket. 'We sell an awful lot more for Australia. They don't have scorecards at home,' says Anderton. Down

Under, spectators rely on large, informative scoreboards, as do growing numbers of the crowd at Lord's.

There will always be a demand for scorecards, however. Not just from collectors, but for members watching in the Committee Room. A scorecard is placed in front of each of the high chairs, like an Order of Service, and swapped for updated cards during the intervals. Some matches have A4 scorecards, but for the Committee Room the cards are 9½" by 5" printed specially, and that's that.

THE BOYS IN THE BACKROOM

Grant Jenkins cuts an unlikely figure at Lord's. He is a social engineer, a man dedicated to the idea that relations between employers and employed can be elevated to a higher plane of efficiency and understanding. He also loves cricket. When headhunters said in 2003 that there was a job going at Lord's he told them they could stop looking. He had played there as a schoolboy at Tonbridge, and for Southern Schools when their games were still fixtures in a Lord's summer. He had even tried out for Kent, but chose instead to do a proper job, settling for club cricket and coaching kids in Berkshire. He is talkative, fit, neatly bearded, and his title is Personnel and Training Manager. But his CV shows time spent as a management consultant and a headhunter as well.

MCC employs 160 men and women and another 30 who are regular casuals. Jenkins notes that only three per cent of British companies have more than 150 employees; in that context, he says, we're quite a sizeable business. When he arrived at Lord's, he did not like what he saw: 'Service excellence is the key at Lord's' but he agreed with David Batts's view that customer service was still lacking. 'A lot of people didn't understand what a customer was.' He watched for a while, and then presented Roger Knight with a plan to create a meritocracy at Lord's. 'We wanted to retain MCC's positive traditions, but to position ourselves in a more commercial environment,' he says.

Poor communication was the problem. 'Real communication is involving people in your thinking.' He set up focus groups, trying to start a conversation with the staff: 'A lot of what we're doing is changing the mindset.' He has seen the future, and thinks it might work. One problem, however, is that there are people at Lord's who fondly remember the past and think that worked. In the days when Lieutenant-Colonel John Stephenson was Secretary at the Old Lord's, his style was admired by Jim Webb, the senior electrician. 'He used to walk around every morning, and if there was a problem, he'd hear of it.' The tension between Old and New, management and labour, means that Lord's is not always a happy ship.

Jenkins wanted 'the good guys' – and the good gals presumably – to be rewarded. 'Instead of everyone getting a three- or four-per cent pay increase, we want the good guys getting nine or ten per cent. Not being good wasn't going to pay.' This was a recipe for uncertainty and disappointment. Old hands suddenly left; there were no fewer than eight casualties in the accounts department in the summer of 2004, a shocking thing in an organisation sometimes unused to decisive management. A couple of bold spirits said the right response was to join a trade union, but that was a step too far for most people, however disenchanted they were. They would have been negotiating from a position of weakness. People who work at Lord's know that a job there is desirable. If they walked out, there would be four or five people wanting to replace them.

Jenkins had no illusions; he expected some trouble. 'There was bad feeling, and in a way, you couldn't blame them. There were a lot of people who weren't prepared to change. It was attitudinal. It could have been anywhere.' But he pressed on with his recommendations for a new 'performance culture', pay structure, incentive scheme and improved pensions.

The new order gets no support from Jim the electrician, who started work at Lord's thirteen years ago. He sits in his room surrounded by miles of wire and cable, wearing an extra large size of the blue sweatshirts with the Lord's logo on the breast, which are worn, appropriately, by the blue-collar workers. The uniform, he observes, distinguishes them from those at Lord's who wear collars and ties. 'It's still a bit like *Upstairs Downstairs*.' In the internal telephone directory he has no name: he is known only as 'Electrician'.

But he still likes the atmosphere: 'it's a nice place to work,' he says. He likes to recall conversations with celebrities such as Brian Johnston, the jolly broadcaster who took refuge from his fans in Webb's workshop. Dickie Bird, umpire and bestselling author, loved the crowds and the ground, but he would stop by to tell stories from his extensive repertoire – like the one about the batsman who walked, saying to Bird, 'I wasn't out, but I want a bet on the next race.'

Webb works from 7.00 a.m. to 7.00 p.m. on big match days, including Sundays during Tests. No overtime (he gets two days in lieu, and for having worked over a weekend during a Test). As an electrician, he is an all-rounder. He replaces light bulbs, and fixes fire alarms; if a trailer in the Food Village blows its generator, he restores the power; if the new air cooling system in the Pavilion is not working, he fixes the computer that operates it. 'We're a necessary evil. Sometimes busy, sometimes not,' he says.

For Webb, who is on the verge of retirement, the chief changes in his time at Lord's are the emphasis on health and safety, and the commercial agenda. 'It's far more money-oriented than it was ten years ago,' he says. He lingers over tales of the old days, when the Colonel's lady offered him breakfast after he had done some emergency electrical work in the Secretary's tied cottage behind the real tennis court ('Where's my breakfast?' the Colonel asked. 'Jim's eating it,' his wife replied). Roger Knight is seen as a different quantity. 'He's like an old schoolmaster with his pupils. We don't really know him,' says Webb.

He feels left out of Jenkins' brave new world. He cannot believe, for example, that it is right for secretaries to be paid as much as craftsmen. Management tell him he gets a fair wage, but he doesn't agree. 'That's what I find frustrating,' he says. The old days of Col. Stephenson suited him best. 'If you'd done wrong, he'd tell you, but he stuck by you through thick and thin. Now you're under pressure all the time.' That is part of the modern management package that Jenkins is offering. Jim Webb is the old. Grant Jenkins is the new.

Most of Webb's maintenance work is done for Jon Hawke, whose title is his job description. As Ground Preparation Manager, he has to ensure that Lord's looks as good as his team can make it. He deals, he says, with everything on the ground that isn't green. 'We treat every fixture the same. One man or 30,000 – there's no difference in the standard as far as we are concerned.' But there is a difference in the job satisfaction. 'Our greatest triumph is at the end of a night when we've cleared away 30 tons of rubbish, and the next morning it looks like nothing had taken place the day before. We get a buzz out of that, because we all know we've done it.'

Hawke was born not far away, in Primrose Hill. His grandfather worked on the gate at Lord's when he retired from the civil service, and got a steward's job during the holidays for his son, Hawke's father, who was a school teacher. Hawke's father in turn got a job for his son. When he was at university, Jon worked as a steward every weekend during the summer. He started on a six-month contract in 1987, and now he lives there, in the middle flat in the red-brick block overlooking the nursery. He is at work as soon as he steps out of the front door. He belongs there; two of his children were born at Lord's.

Like Mick Hunt, his downstairs neighbour, Hawke is busy in the winter. Seats in the Mound Stand have to be covered with black plastic bags, and these are recycled as bin bags at the start of the season. They do not last long: 2,500 of them get filled on big match days. When it is too cold outside, Hawke's squad paints boxes and internal corridors. The major blitz starts six weeks before the start of the season, cleaning the seats, washing down the terraces, painting the stands. There's no point in starting earlier because the seats would get dirty all over again. 'I must be the only person here who likes rain – it washes down the terraces,' says Hawke. When a big paint job is required on the stands, outside contractors are called in. When the Media Centre needs cleaning, which is three times a year, abseilers are hired to shin down the sides of the pod to clean it. Large mechanical cherry pickers are called in to lift the window cleaners up to the sheer glass window overlooking the ground.

During Test matches, Hawke and his men work from dawn till dusk, tidying up after the caterers, on call to fix seats, collecting rubbish throughout the day in the two converted milk floats – known as dillies – and taking it to two compactors. These hold twelve tons each, and are changed each morning. The rest is chucked into an open skip and removed by Westminster Council. On each stand, a man with a mop, a bucket and some sand is on hand – 'in case someone doesn't like what they've eaten for lunch'.

At Old Lord's, the ground was cleaned each night by casual cleaners drawn from London's homeless, old lags and winos who waited for close of play in a ragged row outside the North Gate. Geoffrey Moorhouse described them in his book about Lord's, written in 1983, finding characters like The O'Brien and his nephew Ginger from the County Monahan, and the fearless Ryan Brothers from Belfast. A pair called Cash and Carry shared a tartan tam-o'-shanter, and while one worked, the other looked for unfinished cans and bottles of booze. Benito the Pope spent his earnings in the betting shop rather than the off-licence, which was unusual. Hawke, who was in charge of this motley crew, says that most of them spent the £16 they earned during a four-hour shift on drink. It would, he says, have saved time to pay them in kind.

Now the job is done by 120 neatly dressed young people provided by a cleaning contractor. The old lags were declared redundant soon after 2000, despite the loyalty many of them had felt towards Lord's. Hawke says: 'They wouldn't work at the Oval, some of them. They felt it was beneath them.' Now they are characters in the sentimental story of the Old Lord's. They were victims of MCC's desire to placate local residents, unhappy at these unruly looking figures queuing up at the North Gate every evening during Tests. 'It was felt they had to go,' says Hawke. They did not fit the image of New Lord's, which, as Hawke notes, strives to greater professionalism and commercialism. 'You can't relax now,' he says, but the old ways did not enchant him, as they did Jim Webb. 'When I first started here you were regarded as a club servant rather than an employee. That was the attitude of the time,' says Hawke.

Mind you, disobliging attitudes were not confined to the members.

Hawke recounts with gusto a story told among the staff about gatemen and stewards from the time of his arrival at Lord's. In 1987, MCC celebrated its bicentenary with a five-day match between MCC and the Rest of the World. Unfortunately, the last day was lost in the rain; but the story goes that it was just as well, as the match could not have been played anyway because of staff shortages. The day coincided with the funeral of Nazi war criminal Rudolf Hess, and the gatemen and stewards would naturally be in attendance to pay their respects.

When I repeated this hoary tale to Jeff Cards, the Head Steward, he smiled faintly and shrugged like a man who has heard it many times. 'We've got that reputation. Some of it we deserved. There was a lot of dead wood, and some people liked to live up to the authoritarian image. We've had to become a more professional unit.'

Despite his fresh-faced appearance, Cards is a veteran, having joined MCC in 1986, straight from school. He transferred to the stewards' office three years later, shortly before the sudden departure of the Head Steward, as it turned out. He got that job at the age of 20. Since then he has overseen big changes in personnel and policy in the stewards' department. The greatest change, he says, came after the World Cup in 1999, when stewards were injured and players given a bad scare during pitch invasions. 'After that, the principal obligation was seen as protecting the people playing the game.' Security has steadily increased. There are sniffer dogs at the gates, bags are searched – even those belonging to members – and bodies are scanned. 'It's showing a bit of strength to people who might make trouble.' The one-day game between England and Australia that took place three days after the terrorist bombing in London on 7 July went ahead because MCC was confident that the security operation in place made Lord's as safe against terrorism as any public place holding 30,000 people can be.

Cards starts planning the next season in December. There are 400 stewards on the books, including a core of 40 who are used regularly at Middlesex games and the traditional matches at Lord's. Most of them work only fifteen days a year at Lord's, but they work at sporting events such as

Wimbledon and Ascot as well. 'Stewarding is a little bit of a closed shop,' says Cards. This is why, for a casual occupation, turnover is low. To fill vacancies, he trawls job websites, and is best pleased when he comes across retired police officers.

New stewards attend training course at which they learn about health and safety and 'customer care scenarios'. Cards judges where they will best fit in, because different stands require different personalities. Members prefer quiet, familiar figures. Public stands require more 'robust' stewarding, with people drawn from various ethnic backgrounds. 'We have an excellent mix from all Test nations: Indians, Pakistanis, West Indians. It helps having someone who speaks the lingo.'

The greatest single problem is not drunks or flag-wavers or horn-blowers, but serial users of mobile phones. A mobile phone was given as the cause of a scandalous episode, unique in the history of Lord's, when one MCC member brandished a knife in the Tavern Stand in 2004. He resigned a few weeks later.

On big match days, Cards's stewards are augmented by 70 uniformed men and women from the armed services. Since these soldiers, sailors and airmen are a fixture at Wimbledon, MCC thought it would like to have them too. The Metropolitan Police are a presence; they advise on security, and deal with crime, but Cards notes that, after the Hillsborough disaster, the police took a backward step at sporting events. 'They don't want to get involved too much.'

The heavy, potentially violent work of dealing with pitch invasions and streakers is farmed out to specially trained agency stewards. Cards reveals a trade secret: you don't chase streakers, you surround them, giving them nowhere to go except the boundary, where they are handed over to police. They may or may not be charged with aggravated trespass, which is the worst they can be accused of. In 2004, when total attendances were around 400,000, exactly fifteen spectators were ejected. It was a satisfactory result for Cards.

A CONVERSATION
WITH ROGER KNIGHT

Roger Knight, MCC's Secretary and Chief Executive, occupies one of the most desirable executive offices imaginable. It is at the end of the corridor beyond the visitors' dressing room. It is not a large room. There is a conference table and chairs just beyond the door, a bookcase filled with a long run of leather-bound *Wisden*s, and a desk with a comfortable chair that swivels round to face a keyboard, screen and printer. Beyond the desk is a window with a panoramic view of Lord's, looking across to the plane trees in the churchyard behind the Nursery Ground.

Knight is tall, slim and fit. He was 59 in September 2005, and does not look it – the face is angular, and the figure trim. The son of a public schoolmaster at Dulwich College, Knight followed his father into teaching, becoming a headmaster. He has the manner and mannerisms of his former trade. He is polite, a tolerant disciplinarian, and discreet by nature. He hates, he says, talking about himself. Self-promotion is bad form. But he is generous with his time, and, when the subjects are cricket and MCC, he is in no hurry to bring a conversation to an end.

Knight was a precocious cricketer who played for Surrey when the university term at Cambridge was over. His start in first-class cricket overlapped with Tom Graveney's final flourish. Like other admirers, he recalls Graveney's elegance; unlike the overwhelming majority of them, Knight actually bowled him out. 'I was medium in every respect, but I did make the ball bounce because I was tall, and I could swing it both ways. But I wouldn't have minded batting against my bowling.'

Surrey were playing at Worcester late in the summer when Knight found himself bowling at Graveney: 'I bowled one from wide of the crease and it went straight. He might have got a little nick, and as he went past he said it was the best ball he'd received all season.' Graveney always was a gentle flatterer. *Wisden* records that this exchange took place on 31 August 1968 when Knight was 21 years old: T. W. Graveney b. Knight 23.

When Knight left Cambridge, where he had studied French and German, he did not know whether he wanted to be a schoolmaster or a

Roger Knight. From Headmaster to MCC Secretary and Chief Executive.

VIEW FROM THE LONG ROOM: '*Wednesday 11th and Friday 13th May 2005 – the lovely stewards have kindly let me sit in their chair today. I've had lots of interesting conversations and compliments from everyone passing by, though I must be fairly inconspicuous, as someone asked me what the score was, thinking I was the steward! It's the Middlesex v. Gloucestershire County Championship match, and there are a few brave souls out on the terraces, but we've taken cover from the eager east wind racing across the ground. Shut that door please!!!'*

cricketer. So he became both. He taught at Eastbourne College during the winter and spring, and played county cricket in the summer. But not for Surrey. Since they could not guarantee him a first-team place, he went to Bristol. Gloucestershire said he could start the season at number three, and then it was up to him. He scored 1,000 runs in 1971. 'I never looked back,' he says.

Five years at Gloucestershire were followed by two closer to home at Sussex. At the age of 31, he was contemplating a schoolmaster's life full-time when, to his surprise and delight, he was asked if he would like to captain Surrey. 'I wanted to captain a side. I thought I had some leadership potential.' He also thought he had a chance to play international cricket, though that was not to be. Dulwich College gave him a teaching job when he was not playing cricket. He was still having his cake and eating it.

He played county cricket until 1984, and his final appearance in first-class cricket was for MCC in 1988 against a World XI organised by MCC's *bête noire* Michael Parkinson at the Scarborough Festival. In his career he scored 19,588 runs in first-class cricket, with 31 hundreds and an average of 32.00. He also took 369 wickets at 36.13; for an all-rounder, the record is commendable. Knight is no statistics man himself. He can dredge up a few innings from his memory – highest score, 164 for Sussex against Middlesex; a chancy 60 against Fred Trueman at Hull, but what he remembers best is Colin Cowdrey's footwork, and Peter May's timing, even when he had retired from Test cricket. Cowdrey always greeted Knight when he came to the crease with – 'Good morning, schoolmaster.'

Once retired, Knight became a housemaster at Cranleigh School near Guildford, and went on, as headmaster, to Worksop College in Notting-hamshire. An enthusiastic playing member of MCC since his undergraduate days, he went on tours to Kenya and West Africa. As a French speaker, he was chosen to captain MCC against France in a celebration of MCC's 200th birthday. A generous declaration allowed France to win in the last over. Hubert Doggart, a Lord's grandee and fellow schoolmaster, told him: 'If you're ever a headmaster and you're as generous as that, you'll go under.'

Knight had never been to an annual general meeting when he was elected to the MCC Committee in 1989. Yet, within five years, to his surprise, he was Secretary of MCC, having been asked to apply when Colonel Stephenson retired. He had then been at Worksop for only two years. 'I always thought my cricket was better than my languages,' he says.

A shortlist came down to two, and Knight was chosen. Tim Lamb, the other contender, went to the ECB as Chief Executive. Knight moved into the Secretary's house in Grove End Road, which is reached by a passage that runs by the side of the Middlesex Office. Knight says the only downside was the dog. There were 350 acres in the grounds of Worksop College; now he would have to walk the dog in Regent's Park. (No one informed him that Regent's Park covers 485 acres.)

He started work in 1994, without an agenda, he professes. He is a pragmatist by nature. 'I'm not afraid of committees. In fact I quite like them,' he says. As Secretary, he is responsible to the MCC Committee. As Chief Executive, he manages the staff. On one side, the members; on the other, the staff. The potential for a clash of ideas and responsibilities between amateur and professional streams is considerable. 'My job is to merge them so they all become the same idea. A chief executive from industry would find it very difficult.'

Instead of posing as a figure of authority, Knight became a master of compromise. He thinks that his style has worked. 'I think it's been a natural transition from a committee-led club to an executive-led club.' He adds that the MCC Committee still has the final say on major decisions – such as that of Knight's successor, who will take over in 2006. Reaching compromises takes more time than most chief executives would allow, but Knight is a patient man. 'You put up with repetition, plus people droning on about things you know about.' Close colleagues react differently to this: David Batts finds endless discussion infuriating. Colin Maynard, who knows no other system, finds it easier to tolerate.

'I think it has gone pretty well. There have been difficult moments, and some nicer times.' The good times usually involved a bold new building like the Indoor School, the Grand Stand, or the Media Centre. Bad times were the 'unpleasantness' over the World Cup (some members protested that they should not have to pay to watch any match at Lord's, including the final), and the admission of women members, which twice came to a hotly contested vote of the whole membership. Knight was in favour of it: 'My view is that we are a cricket club, and anyone who played or loved the game, or was in any way involved, should be able to join the club.' Tony Lewis, the President, took the full force of a vituperative attack on MCC's governance. 'I don't think anyone would have coped in those circumstances.'

And after he goes? He speculates about ways of increasing the ground's capacity: a second tier over the Compton and Edrich Stands, a comprehensive redevelopment of the Tavern and Allen Stand, and the Tavern Banqueting Suite. The growth of a compensation culture may force MCC to cease to be a club owned by all its members and become a limited company or a friendly society. This would protect members against the cost of disasters – 'not just terrorism, but, say, food poisoning'.

Knight is proud of MCC's role in university cricket, and of its tours to play cricket in unlikely places, such as Estonia in 2005. 'To a certain extent, we're a playing arm of the ICC,' he says, and he sits on the ICC's development committee. When MCC surrendered authority over international cricket to the ICC, and over domestic and English Test cricket to the ECB, it became introspective for a while; but it found, he says, that MCC was not happy on the outside. 'I think we've established a public role again.'

Regrets? 'We talk about cricket too little. There is a huge danger that we become just a money-making machine,' says the Secretary and Chief Executive.

A DAY OUT IN BRISTOL

MCC teams appeared in no fewer than 37 out-matches in the first full week of July. One of these was at Tom Graveney's old school, Bristol Grammar. He had not been back there for some years, not since he opened the sports hall that was named after him. Now that he had a personal interest in both teams he decided to watch them, and I tagged along.

When he was a schoolboy before and during the Second World War, the playing fields were in a Bristol suburb called Golden Hill. Tesco wanted the site for a supermarket, and made the school an offer it couldn't refuse for most of the land. Subsequently, the cricket fields moved across the Clifton Suspension Bridge to a distant suburb called Failand. Driving through Bristol towards the ground, Graveney pointed out the comfortable house where he had lived when he was a cricketer. He recalled that he had gone on living there when he quit Gloucestershire and played for Worcestershire, satisfying MCC's residential requirements with an accommodation address in Broadway. He never minded bending rules enforced by people he regarded as bureaucrats.

Graveney knew Failand well. He had played golf there, though not as well as his brother Ken. As we strolled on to the terrace in front of a two-storey pavilion, the first person Graveney saw was his great-nephew Adam, son of David Graveney, England's Chairman of Selectors, who is Ken's son. Adam, wearing an MCC tie, is tall and well built. He captains the Old Bristolians' second team, and he had been selected by MCC to help the

President feel at home. Adam calls him 'Uncle Tom'. His mother was there, too; David arrived later. It was a family occasion.

Kevin Blackburn, the school's cricket coach, says cricket is taken seriously at Bristol Grammar School. A good, competitive team, like a decent school orchestra, is a selling-point in the crowded and competitive market for private education. Blackburn gets plenty of help, but there is nothing he can do about the summer exam schedule, which is the bane of school cricket. Fortunately, this fixture comes late in the term, and all his most promising young players are available to test themselves: boys against men.

This was 7 July, and the morning had been punctuated by reports of bombs on the London Underground. But the game began promptly, under a grey sky. The custom is that MCC bat first, before making a well-judged declaration which is designed to produce a result. This also allows MCC batsmen travelling some distance to arrive a bit late.

The match manager, who selects, organises and captains MCC's team, was Gareth Griffiths, a burly, good-natured Bristol man. Despite the remarkable number of games on MCC's fixture list, seventeen players had said they would like to play. Most of them were from the Bristol area, too. MCC sounds like a London club, but the playing members are spread throughout the country. To play as many out-matches as MCC does, they need to be.

Griffiths is from Surrey, but he went to the University of the West of England in Bristol, and liked the city so well that he never left it. He does not let his job selling mortgages interfere with his cricket. Even though he is not an old boy, he captains the Old Bristolians, and he has played for MCC since 2000. Later in the summer he would be a member of MCC's touring party to Finland and Estonia.

Three of MCC's players were Old Bristolians themselves. A couple of them had sons in the school team. Tom Parnell, the school captain, was playing against his father Tim, a former captain of the Old Bristolians. Mike Neale was on one side; his son James on the other. Simon Wickham, a school friend of Griffiths, had come all the way from Reigate. The two of them had bumped into each other at a Lord's Test the previous summer, and agreed to play together in Bristol. Wickham normally represents MCC in Surrey, and always tries to play against a local state school, where he and his colleagues offer advice in the nets, and chart improvements from year to year.

Four of MCC's team were probationary candidates hoping to win Griffiths' approval in his match report to Fraser Stewart at Lord's. Probationers are expected to play a dozen or so games in each of two seasons. Anthony Higgs had driven from north London to get a game. Two were local men – Alex Harris and Darren Roe, an insurance broker in Bristol. Roe says that he would like to prove good enough to qualify for an overseas tour – though the chance to see Tests at Lord's as an MCC member was a plus.

MCC owed their sound start to Harris, who struck the ball well before losing his wicket for 64, but tight bowling meant that runs were not easily come by. Graveney was interested in a young seam bowler who lacked height but not pace. His name is Will Tavaré, and he is a nephew of Chris, England's merciless blocker. A fourteen-year-old leg-spinner called Felix Currell can already turn the ball. 'He'll turn it more,' says Graveney, 'when his hands grow larger and more muscular'. He thought Chris Gwyther, a left-arm spinner, would be a good bowler 'when he gets more body behind his action'.

Three wickets had fallen when Adam Graveney walked to the crease. Griffiths knew he was anxious not to let the family down. His uncle fell silent before Adam received his first ball. He reached far forward on his front foot and played it back to the bowler. 'That's a Graveney for you,' said Tom, reaching out his own front foot. When Adam was out, having hit the ball hard and scored 31, he got an approving, avuncular nod.

Two more wickets fell to splendid catches in the slips and at mid-off, where Gwyther took an athletic diving catch to dismiss Darren Roe, who had done his playing membership application no harm by scoring a thumping 50. MCC declared on 214 for 9; Griffiths, who bats number seven for his club side, did not bat. 'My choice. I wanted everyone else to get a bat,' he says.

Griffiths had one seamer and six spinners in his team, but he thought MCC were safe: 'Generally boys find it harder to cope with men's bowling.' And so it proved. Despite a brave 50 from their captain Tom Parnell, Bristol Grammar School were out for 150. MCC won by 69 runs. Griffiths, an off-spinner, didn't get a bowl either, but his probationers had had a chance to show what they could do; and, like the speaker at a prize day, he declared that the school team were a great deal better than last year.

Over lunch, MCC's players quizzed Graveney about the life of a professional cricketer: the stories flowed effortlessly, recycled for a new audience. He is easygoing, and soon puts at ease the amateur cricketers who sit at his feet. 'Everyone was proud,' says Griffiths, 'of the first professional cricketer to be President of MCC. About time.'

THE CURATOR'S GUIDED TOUR

Adam Chadwick is an exotic at Lord's. At home in pin-striped suits and colourful ties, Chadwick arrived at MCC via Oxford, the Courtauld Institute of Art and Christie's, the auctioneers, where he was head of the department of European decorative arts. At Christie's, he practised the art of persuasion, bringing to the job an instinctive charm and a cheerful smile. He was beginning to tire of the auction trade when a friend mentioned an advertisement in the *Guardian* for the post of curator at MCC, as successor to Stephen Green, who had been 35 years at Lord's, and had written a history of the place.

In Australia, curators are groundsmen. At MCC, the curator looks after historic collections of paintings and books. Chadwick was well qualified for this. He has a good eye, both as a critic and a cricketer. At Oundle School he had opened the batting with Tom Harrison, who played a few games for Derbyshire. His role was 'stolid defender'. When he arrived at Lord's, Chadwick found himself in charge of a small department, answerable to Colin Maynard and the Arts and Library Committee, which runs the Library and the Museum, hangs old paintings and commissions new ones and looks after the tour guides (and, incidentally, commissions books such as this).

Chadwick had not come from a museum background. 'It was a card in my favour, because they were looking for somebody who would move quickly, galvanise things.' One of his first moves was to relocate the little urn containing the Ashes – the most famous single item in the collection

– into its own space on the first floor of the Museum. Then he worried that none of the Museum exhibits, which are dominated by images of the English game, would appeal to school parties that included Indian and Pakistani kids. A photographic portrait of Sachin Tendulkar has been acquired, along with the shirt Sourav Ganguly wore during a monumental one-day match against England in 2003. To illustrate an aspect of the modern game, Chadwick organised an exhibit showing the development of the batsman's helmet. To show the life of a modern cricketer, he wanted a professional cricketer's 'coffin' – to show how much gear he uses. He asked Middlesex for help. Rooting around the storeroom, they came up with two: since they had belonged to Mike Brearley, England's master strategist and captain for the later part of the famous 1981 Ashes series, there was no doubt

THE CHAIRS IN THE LONG ROOM: *'Friday 29th April and Wednesday 11th May 2005 – aah, the hallowed Long Room in all its refurbished splendour – just like one of the rooms in the National Gallery with all the fabulous paintings of the great and good in cricket, and their settings, gazing down upon us. As I sit in one of the wonderful chairs, which are an integral part of the Long Room (so undignified that they have to be evacuated for banqueting occasions), I'm sure that the three gentlemen in the painting just beyond this sketch are wondering who has allowed this woman in here… it is a fabulous painting!'*

about their 'museum quality' – especially as one was decorated with MCC touring stripes.

In the summer of 2005, Chadwick curated an excellent exhibition of photographs titled '33 years and 50 Tests through the lens of Patrick Eagar'. Eagar is the doyen of cricket photographers, and the selection included landscapes of Lord's and photographs of cricketers at play – Compton and Edrich drinking with Hutton and Miller is a classic – as well as action pictures in the middle. Tom Graveney wrote in an introduction to the catalogue: 'The emphasis on change is constant in all but one element. Ashes contests at Lord's.' They have not changed since 1934 – the last time England won.

The greatest treasure at Lord's is the Ashes urn, but it also houses a unique collection of paintings in the Pavilion. Chadwick had been lucky: the refurbishment of the Pavilion meant that there was time to clean and restore the collection, and to rehang it, before the building reopened. He took advice, of course, from members of his committee, but the responsibility was his. He took me on a guided tour, starting in the Long Room.

He had a notion of a Victorian-style hang there, with as many paintings as possible crowding the walls – the way it was once done at the Royal Academy. That would have meant sacrificing symmetry and spacing to a rich diet of colour. Chadwick chose discretion rather than valour, but the idea remains at the back of his mind: 'Fun to do, at some stage.' He chose instead to leave space between good historical paintings – 'as befits the building', he says. It was what the members had come to expect.

His favourite painting is of a Dutch banker's son, called Mr Hope of Amsterdam, playing in Italy, painted by Jacques Sablet, a skilful Swiss portraitist. It shows that you do not have to be a famous cricketer to be worthy of a place in the Long Room. Indeed, the paintings that hang along the long back wall are of anonymous subjects playing cricket early in the history of the game.

Celebrated cricketers hang on the end walls. This is where you find W. G. Grace and Shane Warne. An internal debate about the suitability of Warne was decided in his favour, especially as it was an Ashes summer. Sir Clive Lloyd, Sir Richard Hadlee and Barry Richards represent the relatively modern game at the opposite end, though they appear alongside an unforgettable portrait of the three Victorian gentlemen who founded I Zingari. One, sitting in a bath chair, is wearing a glove knitted in the club colours – red, yellow and black. It was done from a sepia photograph that appears in

Graeme Wright's informative and entertaining collection *Wisden at Lord's*.

Lord's is the subject of the paintings in the Writing Room: 'It's a self-portrait,' says Chadwick. 'There are a couple of pictures that sing in this room, but didn't in the Museum.' One of these is the famous Victorian scene with the Prince of Wales (who became Edward VII) and his mistress at Lord's, much improved by cleaning; another is a painting of Lord's in the 1970s by the Academician William Bowyer. It was, he says, 'looking a lonely soul in the Museum'.

Predictably, the Committee Room is devoted to portraits of figures from MCC's history. The best of them are recent watercolours by John Ward RA. Thomas Lord's portrait, which hangs in the dominant position above the fireplace, is too reverential for Chadwick's taste. 'This is not the wheeling-dealing wine merchant from Thirsk who was willing to sell his ground for his pension. This is a celebration of his achievement in old age. I don't think people walk away from Lord's remembering this picture.' This Lord does not win a place among the first team in the Long Room.

Chadwick's thinks that the best cricket portraits are painted while the sitter is still playing, or soon after. This rule is tested in the members' bar behind the Long Room, which is devoted to paintings of great cricketers in recent history. It is the most controversial room in the Pavilion. There is no debate about the subjects. Keith Miller, Sir Len Hutton, Denis Compton, Sir Don Bradman, Douglas Jardine, Graham Gooch and Sir Garry Sobers – all are great cricketers, though Jardine's credentials are not universally accepted. Chadwick judges them differently. Some are 'pretty poor paintings', others are 'rather good'. They sum up the collection as a whole, he says.

He declares Gooch to be good, as is Sobers and Bradman. The bad paintings are Compton, Hutton, Jardine, and Miller, who, like Bradman, was painted long after he retired. Yet the good ones cause the controversy.

Chadwick originally had a low opinion of the Bradman portrait when he first hung it in the no-man's land between the staircase and the members' bar. He changed his mind when the original decorative scheme for the bar altered and made space for Bradman there. He notes that the bar now

Shane Warne, looking deceptively angelic, poses with artist Fanny Rush.
His portrait was hung in the Long Room during the Ashes Test.

MCC Chairman Charles Fry at the
unveiling of the portrait of Shane Warne.

contains both major players in the Bodyline series – united finally in death, and in paint.

The subjects for new paintings are chosen by the Arts and Library Committee, which dictates that grandees such as presidents should be remembered by photographic portraits in the committee dining room. Only the Secretary gets a painted portrait. Posthumous subjects are not eligible; nor are cricketers in old age. Chadwick declares the new portrait of Shane Warne a success because it was done at the right time – when he is playing. A newspaper story that the portrait had been sent back for amendment (specifically to make his private parts less prominent) offended Chadwick, not just because it was untrue, but because that is not the way the commissioner of a portrait ought to behave: 'You don't become too involved while it is being painted; and when it is finished, never.' Brian Lara is another obvious candidate for a portrait, but there are not many others. Committees are not good at agreeing on deserving subjects. Moreover, if the subjects are playing Test cricket, they find it hard to fit in a series of sittings, if that is what the painter requires.

Chadwick's job is to choose the painter. In search of memorable work, he applies high standards. 'One doesn't want an artist who is reasonably competent, just because he costs only £6,000. You go to an artist who excites you, and is not just representational.' This is a recipe for controversy, and Chadwick is willing to fight his corner. Some of the paintings he likes the best – such as those of Gooch and Sobers – provoke the fiercest denunciations from members. Chadwick replies with a smile. It will be interesting to see if anyone tries to wipe it off his face.

Trawling the Archives

The theory that MCC's red and yellow club colours derive from a nineteenth-century bottle of Nicholson's gin originates with Glenys Williams, who is the archivist at Lord's. But the evidence is circumstantial. To prove the theory beyond doubt would, she says, be her biggest achievement as an archivist. She has worked at Lord's ever since graduating from Sheffield University seventeen years ago. Col. Stephenson, then the Secretary, gave her a day off a week to complete her M.Phil. thesis, 'A Social History of Cricket'. 'It's my home,' she says of Lord's. But that does not mean that she swallows whole the manners, the ethos and the attitudes of MCC. As a social historian she is, by her own admission, more Marqusee than Birley. Mike Marqusee is a Marxist who includes Engels and Trotsky in the bibliography of *Anyone but England* – his attack on the cricket establishment and Sir Derek Birley, author of *A Social History of English Cricket*, is a radical, but less ideologically driven, social historian.

Williams sits on the second floor of the real tennis building, outside the curator's office, at a cluttered desk with shelves of filing boxes behind her. The boxes, labelled with subjects such as SA 68 and SA Tour 70, were once housed, for want of anywhere else to put them, in the photocopying room in the Pavilion. She went in there one day and discovered that the boxes had disappeared. 'If I'd been half an hour later, they'd have been in the incinerator.' Some MCC documents, such as minutes of meetings of various committees, are on microfilm, and can be consulted in the library – after 30 years have passed. She makes researchers welcome. 'We've never turned anyone away' – even when MCC is likely to be embarrassed by the outcome, as it was when Peter Oborne wrote about MCC's role in the D'Oliviera Affair.

The rest of the archive, much of it still uncatalogued, is in those boxes, or in a box room on a half-landing on the way to the library. The lack of space and order perturbs her. 'It's harder to track down material from two years ago than from one hundred and two,' she says. When she arrived, Williams told MCC the archive needed a dedicated space. Apart from finding somewhere to put it, her problem was that the archive, unlike the Museum or the Lord's tours, has no specific budget, and she tends to get caught in the pull between tradition and commerce.

To see what the archive might reveal, I set Williams a test. In his playing days, Tom Graveney was twice in conflict with MCC, about a special registration to allow him to leave Gloucestershire and play for Worcester-shire, and over the ban for playing in a benefit game during a Test match. Williams could turn up nothing from the Test ban, but the minutes of the MCC Committee in May 1961 included references to the refusal of the registration committee to allow him to move immediately, and the rejection of Graveney's appeal against the decision.

This encouraged Williams to search a separate file called 'Meetings at Lord's'. There, a document, dated 4 May and marked 'Confidential' is the memorandum of Graveney's appeal against the decision, taken on 6 April and by a majority 4 to 1, that he must follow the twelve-month residency rule before joining Worcestershire. It is the sort of discovery that justifies the archive.

It tells, from Graveney's viewpoint, the story of Gloucestershire's decision in November 1960 to replace him as captain with a young amateur named C. T. M. Pugh. The cast list is drawn from an old England. There were three fine amateur players on the appeal committee – D. J. Insole, T. N. Pearce, and C. H. Palmer – but it was led by three MCC grandees: Sir William Worsley, that year's President; Lord Cornwallis and Viscount Portal. In the evidence from Gloucester, there are contributions from the Duke of Beaufort, the President, club chairman Sir William Grant and Sir Percy Lister, chairman-designate. In this social context, there must have been a tendency to treat professional cricketers like club servants.

Graveney learned from a phone call on 15 November 1960 of the plan to replace him as captain. The following day he met Lister who had a remark-able tale to tell.' He informed Graveney that the club had suffered a deficit of £13,000 in 1960, and 1960 might, therefore, be the last year for the club.' Lister claimed that they needed a change of captain, and mentioned the name of a man Graveney admired – C. J. – 'Charlie' – Barnett, who was captain when Graveney first played for the county, and was now 49 years old. In the circumstances, Graveney agreed to write a letter of resignation.

By the next day, however, he had changed his mind. He felt he had been badly treated and was disinclined to renew his contract, and this was the day before he learned from a journalist that he was to be replaced, not by Barnett but by an amateur named Tom Pugh. The Duke offered to act as mediator, and there was talk of an offer of £1,000 a year to carry on. Graveney said he was prepared to accept, but no offer came in the post.

On 15 December, Grant let slip that it had been decided two years earlier that an amateur captain would be appointed. Under Graveney, Gloucestershire had finished 2nd and 8th in the Championship. Graveney then made a public statement about the decision to give him the captain's job in those circumstances: when the county knew all the time that he would be replaced by an amateur.

Graveney formally resigned on 5 January, and asked the club to release him so that he could play for another county. On 17 February, his employer seemed to have done the decent thing. A letter from the club secretary, G. H. G. Thomas, told him that the club council had considered his request, and they had 'resolved that an absolute release be granted to T. W. Graveney and consent given to his Special Registration to any county applying for the same.' Worcestershire were given the all-clear to negotiate directly with Graveney, and offered him £750 a year, which he was about to accept.

The reason why everything then changed utterly is not explained, but on 22 February, the Secretary of MCC received a letter from Thomas which ignored the club council's decision. Thomas wrote that every effort had been made to retain Graveney's services for the club. While it was true that the council had consented to his immediate release, Thomas wrote, Graveney had been offered £1,000 a year to stay. (Graveney claimed not to know of the offer.) On 24 February, Worcestershire formally applied for Graveney's special registration. The application was denied, and the appeal process begun.

The appeal committee did not go into detail. The memorandum said: 'They have given the fullest consideration to this representation.' And had decided to ignore it, completely. All that seemed to count was Gloucestershire's claim that they had done all they could to keep Graveney. If that was the case, he was not a free agent and could not move.

This paper from the Lord's archive shows vividly who wielded power at MCC 50 years ago, and how. Glenys Williams's study of cricket's social history had convinced her that 'cricket needed to move into the twentieth century before the twenty-first century was upon us.' The denial of Tom Graveney's freedom to play for another county shows how far there was to go.

In the summer of 2005, Williams received news which could only be interpreted as a win for tradition over the pull of commerce. When the ICC left Lord's for Dubai, office space became vacant in the north clock tower behind the Compton Stand. The consequent game of departmental musical chairs meant the Marketing Department vacated a spacious room behind the squash courts, down a corridor from the library.

This was the ideal location for MCC's archive. When Williams learned in mid-August that it would indeed be used for that purpose, she felt like squatting in the space, so that no one could take it away from her. Shelving was discussed; there would be space for the microfiche machines. This was her chance to catalogue the whole collection at last. Who knows what might turn up? Maybe the minutes of the disciplinary board that ended Graveney's Test career.

MAKING THE LAWS

One year after the Marylebone Cricket Club was founded in 1787, it produced a revised version of the Laws of Cricket, and having done so, assumed responsibility for them. It is remarkable how little the Laws have altered – overarm bowling and declarations are the two significant changes. There has, however, been a constant conversation about the state of the Laws for 217 years. It still takes place at Lord's on the Laws Working Party, a sub-committee of the Cricket Committee. This is where the Laws are interpreted and, if necessary, rewritten. In keeping with the fact that MCC is a club, new Laws are referred to the members for approval at the annual general meeting. In keeping with the reality of modern cricket, approval by the members is taken for granted.

Late in 2004, the Australian umpire Darrell Hair took me to a box in the Grand Stand where the Laws Working Party was to meet to discuss big issues, such as chucking, and small ones, such as overthrows. Hair had recently been appointed MCC Laws Advisor. This confirmed umpires as the most influential members of the Working Party (Nigel Plews, the English first-class umpire, was another member). There was a distinguished grammarian, to keep an eye on the niceties of punctuation, and an observer from the ICC. Roger Knight was chairman. Rachel Lee, who is the Working Party's secretary, is an umpire herself. Although he was entitled to, Tom Graveney did not attend.

He would already have known that umpires are nit-pickers by nature, and nits were ruthlessly picked as they laboured over the complex relationship between cricket's Laws and its traditions. You will find no indication in the Laws, for example, that the bowler must not run out a batsman backing up at the bowler's end without warning him first that he is out of his ground. The warning is a tradition. If the bowler says nothing and whips off the bails, Clause 15 of Law 42 is perfectly clear. It's out.

The ICC had reported to MCC its concern about runs scored from overthrows when a fielder's throw is accidentally deflected by a batsman out of the reach of another member of the fielding side. Some batsmen do not take advantage of the fielder's misfortune, but that is only a tradition. At the Oval Test in 2003, they recalled, India's ninth wicket pair took two runs in just those circumstances. There is no Law against it; and to make one, as the ICC wished to do, was fraught with complications. The easiest way out was to do nothing, but they were not completely comfortable with that: 'I think we know what we mean, but will everyone else? It still needs looking at,' said one member.

There was no doubt about the problem of batsmen running down the middle of the wicket, roughing it up to give their own bowlers an advantage. The Law is clear: there is a protected area five feet in front of the wicket and inside a corridor one foot wide of both the off and leg stump. Umpires had asked the Working Party for guidance, or a more explicit directive; one member wondered whether the protected area should be made larger. Most were unmoved. 'A Law's a Law,' they said.

They had also been asked to comment on the introduction of a fourth stump, presumably to alter the balance of power between batsmen and bowlers. The questions suggested that the proposal would not be taken seriously – 'Could stump manufacturers cope with demand? What about the bails?' The conclusion was magisterial. 'MCC does not anticipate any change in the Law.'

A proposed text for the MCC website's guide to the laws was subjected to detailed grammatical analysis by Sheila Hill, deputy head of St Paul's Girls' School. 'Is the comma in the right place? Is it "s apostrophe", or

"apostrophe s?" Is it "interruption to" or "interruption of"? Should it read "strikers being caught" or "the striker to be caught"?' Tony Lewis, chairman of the Cricket Committee, would sympathise with all this. He was a student of the eminent Cambridge historian J. H. Plumb, who taught him that, by moving a comma in a sentence, you can change the whole meaning of history.

Since the new website would make access to MCC's advice on the Laws so much easier, the Working Party wanted to know who should be permitted to use it. An English umpire said: 'To come to MCC is a big thing. It's going to God, isn't it?' But should anyone from any team from anywhere in the world be allowed to address a question to this august authority? Some of the questions asked are plain daft. One umpire recalls being asked

...ladesh on their first tour to England and the 'home of cricket'. Today I've been beamed up to another world – into the big eye that looks down over everything otherwise known as the Natwest Media Centre. If you can get in here – and you have to have a good...

Karen Neale sept 2005

DO NOT LEAN ON THE GLASS

VIEW FROM THE MEDIA CENTRE: *'Thursday May 26th 2005 – it's the first day of the npower Test Match between England and Bangladesh, on their first tour to England and 'the home of cricket'. Today I've been beamed up to another world – into the big eye that looks down over everything, otherwise known as the Natwest Media Centre. If you can get in here – and you have to have a good reason, famous cricketers past and present, as well as all the journalists are up here – then the view is fantastic, the food is fabulous and you feel like a king (or in my case a queen), and in the main hub here, it's all a buzz to see how poor old Bangladesh will last for...'*

whether a bowler is allowed to run in, turn his back on the batsman, and bowl the ball over his head? The official answer is yes; but, says Hair, if you can't see where you are bowling, what is the point? Common sense dictates that the question is pointless.

Hair's advice was that MCC should not seek to be exclusive. Rather, they should embrace the whole world of cricket. 'I've got no problem with anyone, anywhere, asking a question. There's no such thing as a silly question.' Since it is his job to answer questions, discussion ended there. The state of play is that all cricketers are entitled to ask questions regarding the interpretation of the Laws – via email at laws@MCC.org.uk – if they choose. However, there are a couple of characteristic limitations to this right. From the Preface to the Laws: 'The incident on which ruling is required must not be merely invented for disputation but must have actually occurred in play', and more sternly: 'The enquiry must not be connected in any way with a bet or wager'.

Darrell Hair, who was 52 in the summer of 2005, is an imposing figure, with an Australian accent. As a working member on the ICC's list of elite Test umpires, he is a familiar figure behind the stumps at the bowler's end at a Test. He remains a controversial figure, however, having been left off the original ICC elite list because he was the man who dared to call Muttiah Muralitharan, the second-highest wicket-taker in Test history, for chucking in 1995.

He disappears for 50 or 60 days to umpire Tests and ODIs. Not long before the Working Party met early in September 2005, he was back from Bulawayo, where he had umpired Zimbabwe's game against New Zealand. He confesses that he does not spend his evenings talking to colleagues about the Laws of Cricket. 'It's the last thing you want to do. It's important to relax and take your mind off the job.' But he carries the experience back with him to Lord's to inform the business of the Working Party.

MCC did not advertise when it decided that a figure with international experience was required to become Law Consultant. Hair was hired to train English umpires, as well as to scrutinise the Laws, and he moved to Lincoln, where his wife, who is English herself, had been appointed chief executive of Lincolnshire Enterprise: 'A proper job – not like an umpire,' he says.

Having played in Sydney grade cricket, as a useful fast bowler, he started umpiring when he was 34. Two years later he stood in his first first-class game; he was a Test umpire at 39. 'The more matches you do, the quicker they'll form an idea of your ability,' he says. The right personality is part of the equipment. Hair is confident about his opinions without being dogmatic, unexcitable, even a little dour; and he has no illusions about a Test umpire's vulnerability to vituperative criticism.

As a man with a foot in two camps, he can be trusted when he declares that cricketers round the world readily accept MCC as the lawmaker, and that the only alternative body – the ICC – is happy with that. 'They're aware that it's an area they don't necessarily want to dabble in.' ICC makes Playing Conditions for Test cricket, such as that allowing a bowler to flex his bowling arm up to 15 degrees. MCC makes Laws such as stating what kind of reinforcement on a bat is permitted.

The ICC had introduced new Playing Conditions to cope with chucking in Test cricket. The principal problem is the 'doosra', the off-spinners' leg-break – and, in particular, its use by Muralitharan and the Indian spinner Harbhajan Singh. The ICC had just announced a new Playing Condition that allows a 15-degree tolerance off a straight line in the delivery arm. Co-incidence, no doubt, but this had let Muralitharan off the hook. (It was 14 degrees, in his case.) The ICC had effectively rewritten the chucking Law, and had done so unilaterally, with no reference to MCC.

When he is umpiring a Test, Hair executes ICC Playing Conditions. When he is with the Working Party, he is guided by the Laws. On chucking, the two were no longer the same. What to do? Hair himself thinks an umpire does not need super slow-motion technology to know when a bowler chucks the ball. He believes he can tell just by looking.

The Working Party toyed with ideas that might embrace both the Law and the Playing Conditions, but this was one circle that would not be squared. The ICC could introduce the 15-degree rule because Test umpires have ready access to video footage of every Test player. This would not be available to other first-class umpires, never mind the leagues and club competitions.

The ICC's conclusion seemed contradictory. Despite their change to the Playing Conditions, they declared that Law 24, clause 5 (Definition of fair delivery – the arm) was fine as written. The Working Party also concluded that was nothing to be gained from rewriting the Law. But Roger Knight felt they had not heard the last of the matter. The problem of chucking was not likely to go away.

Ever since MCC first wrote the Laws, manufacturers of cricket equipment have been trusted to conform to them. This has now become big business on a global scale, much of the equipment being mass produced on the Indian sub-continent. Heavy competition was tempting them to produce gloves and bats that bumped up against the Laws. The 'keepers' gloves, for example, may legally have webbing between the thumb and the index finger, but it must not protrude beyond a straight line joining the top of the index finger to the top of the thumb. The webbing must remain taut when the thumb is fully extended. In other words, a pouch is illegal.

It was common knowledge that some manufacturers' catalogues were advertising an illegal version. The problem was that most 'keepers' gloves are imported from India and Pakistan; and these gloves were already on the market. The manufacturers were reluctant to change them: MCC insists that they must. 'Otherwise everyone will be wearing baseball mitts, turning hard chances into easy catches,' said one of the Working Party's umpires.

Then there was the case of Ricky Ponting's bat. The Law is clear enough. 'The blade of the bat shall be made solely of wood', and shall not be more than four and one-quarter inches 'at the widest part'. The sole concession is that the bat may be protected by a very thin, invisible plastic covering. The back of the blade of the bat Ponting used in the Ashes series displayed a green and black graphite strip. This is described by the bat-makers, Kookaburra, as 'reinforcement', and their marketing men promoted the idea that the bat had a bigger 'sweet spot', and would hit the ball harder. MCC fears that the strip introduces an artificial element to the bat. Tony Lewis and Tom Graveney are golfers; both are acutely aware that titanium in driving clubs substantially increases the distance a ball travels. This makes them seriously popular among golfers.

The fear is shared at the ICC. Malcolm Speed, the chief executive, says: 'The last thing that the sport wants is that, at some point in the future, the equivalent of golf's titanium driver is introduced without a full and proper debate.' When ICC announced that Ponting could use his bat while MCC studied the problem, both Kookaburra and Ponting's agent asked what MCC had to do with the case. Speed dealt firmly with that. 'Ensuring that new designs and technologies used in bat manufacture are in keeping with the Laws is exactly what MCC should be doing.'

The impact of the graphite strip is still uncertain. The same technology is used in hockey sticks, and is said to make the ball go faster. Kookaburra, contradicting their marketing men, now says the strip gives no advantage – in which case why bother with it? The lawmakers' concern, however, is that the bat must be made solely of wood. With a graphite strip at the back of the blade, this is no longer the case. Ponting's bat would, then, seem to be illegal. But MCC took legal advice, and their lawyers thought they could resist any challenge from a bat-maker to this interpretation in the courts.

The ICC then set up a sub-committee of their Cricket Committee to determine whether a bat with a graphite strip hit the ball harder, and found a new dimension to the case. Ponting's coloured strip covered the back of the bat, and a coloured bat could be exploited by sponsors. At present, they are limited to a small area on the wooden surface. A bat wholly coloured – in Vodafone red, say – would make a mockery of the Law.

Roger Knight wondered whether the wording of the Law should emphasise the blade's wooden colour. Darrell Hair thought it was time to open a dialogue with equipment manufacturers. Tony Lewis, as chairman of the Cricket Committee, considered appointing a special sub-committee to study new design and technology in bat-making. These are deep waters. MCC still finds them invigorating.

FROM WEST OF WATFORD

E. W. Swanton, one of the grandest of grandees, declared that Tony Lewis was the first MCC President from West of Watford. The sub-text was that Lewis was a provincial chap, from Wales, who had not gone to public school. The witticism was a put-down. Lewis, who went to Neath Grammar School, does not take offence. He was an ambitious boy, a good musician and fine cricketer who got to Cambridge. Cricket became his means of advancement. He captained Glamorgan, and played nine Tests for England, eight of them as captain.

He became an able sports journalist, had his own programme on Radio 4 and wrote books, including *Double Century*, the bicentenary history of MCC. He was welcomed into the fold at Lord's. It was a position he aspired to. 'I believe in aspiration,' he says. 'I believe in the chap with no arse in his trousers and no soles on his shoes having a clear way, if he can play. There's got to be a way through for everyone to enjoy membership.'

He would like to see a kind of egalitarianism through cricket, in which candidates can be judged for fitness for membership on cricket ability and congeniality, not class. This is how MCC members are recruited for out-matches. Those are the people he admires – 'the guys who get up at ten past five in the morning to get to the game by eleven.' Not that many bare-arsed, shoeless candidates may get elected, but you know what he means.

His manner is open and friendly. When we talked over lunch in the Tavern, I asked whether MCC has rid itself of its upper-middle-class image, and become less elitist? 'I thought at first, in an idealistic moment, that it was more user-friendly. But I don't think it is. I think a lot of people join in order to be elitist.' He is not one of the cricket-orientated MCC members who disdain the new commercialism at Lord's. He and David Batts are old acquaintances from when they both ran tourist boards. 'He's a good appointment – a sunny character, with fresh views from outside.'

Lewis succeeded Ted Dexter as chairman of the Cricket Committee, and began to alter the balance of power. One MCC old codger observed that, in his own days on the Cricket Committee, he was the only member who had not captained England. Of the present committee, only Lewis himself and Rachael Heyhoe Flint are former England captains. 'We have avoided the great and the good, which is not surprising for a Welsh grammar-school boy. We have a range of people with something to offer,' says Lewis. For instance, women's cricket is on Lewis's agenda: 'You don't need Geoffrey Boycott to talk about that.' The problem is that young women are not as clubbable as young men. If MCC want more women to play for their team, they will have to go and recruit them. 'We've got to be evangelistic,' says Lewis.

Lewis's missionary instinct is strong. He thinks that MCC cannot be an island unto itself. On the contrary, it has wider responsibilities, at home and abroad. The decision to fund and mentor university cricket has been 'a brilliant success'. He believes that MCC Young Cricketers have shown themselves in the same class as MCC Universities. He speculates about a partnership with a college at London University, and transforming MCC Young Cricketers into London UCCE. As undergraduates, they would be reading cricket.

The next big decision at Lord's is whether to spend a large sum of money on drop-in pitches, but even that has wider implications. These pitches are laid and then prepared away from the field of play on the Nursery Ground in a pitch-sized tray which can be lifted by a powerful loader and transported to a similarly sized hole in the square. They are used at the Melbourne Cricket Ground and in New Zealand, where they are essential because cricket ovals are also used by rugby footballers.

Three experimental drop-in pitches were laid in a corner of the Nursery Ground in 2003. Two used an Australian recipe for the soil content, and one was laid to Mick Hunt's specifications. They were tested in 2004, but the first real workout was in the summer of 2005. Lewis watched county cricketers play on these pitches in the nets for three hours, and thought that they were like Berry Bros' cheap claret – Good Ordinary. Hunt's proved the best soil mixture. But, by the end of the season, Lewis and his colleagues decided that all three ought to be re-laid, on a different base. They were taking their time.

Lewis's committee had talked long and hard about these pitches before accepting the concept in principle. But their condition was that drop-in pitches should not be used in the middle of the square, where the Test pitches are laid. Any upheaval would take place only at the edge of the square. 'We're going into it on very little evidence' says Lewis 'but I think the committee will be quite happy if we give the members more cricket.' Lewis's second reason for going ahead was that MCC can experiment on behalf of all the county grounds in England and Wales where drop-in pitches might work, but where there is not enough money to fund the experiment. It counts as MCC missionary work.

When he became chairman, Lewis brought the Laws Working Party, which had had a degree of independence, back into the bosom of the Cricket Committee. After all, the Laws have global impact, as in the case of Ponting's bat. Lewis had observed an earlier attempt to alter the composition of the bat in Australia, when Dennis Lillee tried to use an aluminium bat; now his concern was based on his knowledge of golf. 'First thing I did was to consult the Royal and Ancient Golf Club in St Andrews – the rule-making body for golf as we are for cricket. The fact is that the moment you allow latitude in preparation of material, you're in the area that golf is in. All because of one decision – to allow metal woods.' (Metal 'woods' enable golfers to drive the ball further.)

Finding a solution will require the judgement of Solomon from Lewis and his colleagues, but he knows how it ought to be done. 'The great thing is to go in with an open mind. Someone could say to me that Ponting's bat is too powerful, but I could, in turn, raise the issue of the weight of bats – which have been getting much heavier. Bringing in the boundary rope, as they did in the Ashes Test at Edgbaston, also distorts the game. I would like to get the balance right between bat and ball,' says Lewis, at his most aspirational.

AN EASY-GOING STEWARD

Eric Dawson became a steward at Lord's because he couldn't get a ticket for the Second Test of England's series against the West Indian tourists in 1957. A friend he had met in the RAF, who was working at Lord's, introduced him to the Head Steward. He asked whether Dawson would like to get paid to watch his team? He became a part-time steward there and then, and worked at weekends. He stayed for 47 years, until his retirement in 2004, and he is still a familiar figure inside Lord's. Walking round the ground, wearing a tweed jacket, a tie and a brown trilby, he is stopped by former colleagues, some of whom hug him so hard his hat nearly falls off. At the bar, payment for his morning cup of coffee is declined. His face, which looks as it has been carved from a piece of dark wood, belongs to that of a patriarch, and he behaves a bit like one. Ask why his role at Lord's was special, and he replies: 'I've got personality, and good manners.' He might add a sweet nature too.

Tom Graveney and Dawson remember that 1957 Test clearly. 'Eric knows a lot about that match,' says Graveney, 'but I know more because I was in it, and got a duck.' So he did: lbw b. Gilchrist; but England won easily. Dawson, who was daft about cricket, then followed his team to see the next Test at Trent Bridge, where Graveney got 258, his highest Test score – though England could only draw. A decade later, Dawson watched Graveney's 151 against India's spinners – the innings he claims as his best at Lord's: 'It was brilliant, flawless. His style was so fluent,' says Dawson. Three England

166

batsmen have really impressed him: Peter May and Colin Cowdrey also, but Graveney is top of his list.

When the engineering firm he had worked for 30 years moved to Scotland in 1985, Dawson's job at Lord's became permanent. He worked in the Indoor School in the winter, and then in the Pavilion, before taking on the job he liked best – steward in charge of the Mound Stand. He did not like the old Mound Stand: under its low roof, he felt claustrophobic. The dashing new Mound Stand with its tented roof is much more to his taste. 'I love it,' he says.

When he was a boy in Jamaica, Dawson's idol was George Headley, the 'Black Bradman'. Dawson was a club cricketer, an all-rounder who batted left-handed at number four, and bowled leg-breaks mainly, though he could also bowl off-breaks. Headley coached at his local club and one evening Dawson was bowling off-breaks in the nets. Headley took the bat and said he would show them how to play spin. Instead of a predictable off-break, Dawson delivered a leg-break instead, and bowled the great man. Headley was spitting mad. 'Cricket is a discipline thing,' he shouted. 'You must always obey your captain.'

'Yes, Massa George,' Dawson replied. You can still hear that West Indian lilt.

He emigrated to New York City, which he did not enjoy ('much too fast'). Besides, there was no cricket. In 1952, Dawson arrived in London, and within months he was doing National Service in the RAF. He had hoped to play professional cricket in Lancashire, but could get no job. The pleasure he had from cricket came from watching it, and rubbing shoulders with the great men of the game.

He bought cigarettes for Sir Len Hutton. When the three of them were sitting together, Keith Miller mischievously asked Dawson whether he or Neil Harvey was the better friend. ('I was not going to answer'). He liked Ken Barrington – 'even though he was Surrey.' Mike Brearley, 'a gentleman', always asked to see Dawson if he was in a Mound Stand box. When Denis Compton received a CBE instead of the knighthood Dawson believed he deserved, Dawson was offended. He tapped a bemused Compton on each shoulder, saying 'Arise, Sir Denis'. 'He nearly fell off his chair.'

THE PLAYERS' BALCONY:
'*Saturday 3rd September and Wednesday 7th September 2005 – two lovely sunny days for the Cheltenham and Gloucester Trophy Final to a packed audience and also the first day of the Middlesex versus Kent Frizzell County Championship match, and here I am sat once more in the privileged Pavilion sneaking a glance across to the 'away' team's balcony. Both up close and from afar, Mr Verity has designed a real beauty of a building in all its warm and welcoming hues…*'

Sir Paul Getty, the great philanthropist whose money had made the new Mound Stand possible, had his own box there, and they liked each other. When Getty invited Dawson and his wife to Wormsley, his cricket ground in the country, he always sent a car and a chauffeur to drive them there and back. 'He knew I loved champagne,' says Dawson, 'and he didn't want me to drink and drive.'

The transition from the old Lord's to the new could not happen fast enough for Dawson. When he first worked there, most of the secretariat were ex-servicemen, and they ran Lord's as if the staff were subject to military discipline. As for the members, he thought they were too strait-laced, and said so. 'I said to Peter May that I'd like to see them a bit mellower.' Peter May later quoted Dawson's remark at an annual general meeting. The mellowing process has been gradual. 'But they start to relax, and that is nice.'

In the Mound Stand, Dawson tried to see that friendliness was not stifled by the officious application of the regulations: 'I was allowed to use my discretion, but I used it in an honourable fashion.' This easy-going attitude did not endear him to all his colleagues. 'One of the security guys at the gate, noticing a few people were passing and saying "hello Eric", said: "I've noticed you've buttered up a lot of people in this place." I said to him: "Look, you've got to work with people not against people. You've got to learn to use your discretion." ' The thought still does not occur to many gatemen.

Dawson remembers the hard times when MCC wondered where it would find the money to redevelop the public stands. Without branding and marketing, he says, MCC would still be worried about having enough money. He approves of the commercialisation of Lord's. If he had his way, though, Test cricket would still be run by MCC.

When the painter Jocelyn Galsworthy compiled a book of portraits of figures in the game, she called it 'Lords of Cricket: Players, Personalities, Legends.' Eric Dawson never qualified as a player, but there is no doubt that he is a personality, and he may be on the way to becoming a legend at his old place of work, so she included him.

PRELUDE TO A LORD'S TEST

The Lord's Test is a cricket festival in a big city. It is party time, with some instruction added to the entertainment before the start. Inspired by MCC's 'Spirit of Cricket' campaign, the instruction takes the form of the Cowdrey Lecture. Begun in 2001 in memory of Colin Cowdrey, the lecture is delivered two days before the Test. Much of the preparatory work for the lectures is done by Laura Garland, the Deputy Head of Communications, and Mark Nicholas, who regularly chairs the question-and-answer session which follows. The lecture itself is delivered by a very good former cricketer who has ideas about improving the game. Richie Benaud, in his lecture, sought to encourage batsmen to walk when they knew they were out. Sunil Gavaskar wanted to discourage predatory and obscene sledging.

The first four lecturers had been from overseas, MCC wanted an Englishman in 2005. Their choice was surprising because during his playing days the lecturer had made mischief at Lord's. Since then, Geoffrey Boycott had become a controversial figure, in and out of the TV commentary box. Iain Wilton, the Head of Communications, said later: 'We're not going just for people with squeaky-clean reputations.' Boycott himself had been alerted to the idea the previous year; and when he was formally offered the lecture early in 2005, he accepted eagerly. He and Cowdrey had not been friends, but he felt real affection for MCC, which had asked him to become an honorary life member before his own Yorkshire county club did.

The lecture, delivered in the Nursery Pavilion on Tuesday evening, is lit by TV lights, and members of the audience at the back crane their necks to glimpse the participants on a screen behind the podium. This year, the extended Cowdrey family were guests of honour. Tom Graveney made a gradual progress up the aisle, stopping – deliberately I thought – for a chat with a former committee member named John Fingleton, who had resigned reluctantly for personal reasons. Introducing Boycott, he recalled that they had put on 120 together at Lord's in Graveney's comeback innings of 96 in 1966. He turned to Boycott for confirmation. Boycott nodded. 'I knew he'd know,' said Graveney, about a man who can give the impression that he knows everything about cricket.

Boycott began with flattery. 'Tom Graveney was my boyhood hero,' he said. Why not his fellow Yorkshireman Len Hutton? Because on the two occasions he had been taken to Bradford to see him, it had rained. The

Former England and Yorkshire batsman Geoffrey Boycott delivers the Cowdrey Lecture. He advocated drastic measures to save Test cricket.

subsequent lecture explained how to save Test cricket: 'Unless we get more fans and spectators in the grounds, Test cricket will die in the years to come.' On the face of it, this seemed unlikely. Like other English Test grounds, Lord's would be packed for the first four days of the Ashes series. But Boycott emphasised that he was not talking about England, nor Sydney, Melbourne or Cape Town. Elsewhere, audiences for Tests are falling. Boycott's solution? Four-day Tests of seven hours a day, with fifteen overs an hour, and day/night Test cricket. 'We need to concentrate the action without losing any of the skills.'

Boycott's principal target was the ICC. Giving Test status for Zimbabwe and Bangladesh was 'an embarrassment'. On making TV technology available to umpires: 'I want more, not less.' Throwing? 'I'm one of those ex-players who think you either bowl with a straight arm, or you don't.' He made it abundantly clear that he thinks Muttiah Muralitharan doesn't.

Graveney thought Boycott had been good value: 'He puts over his points complete with the answers,' he said. Then, he and Boycott, the Cowdrey clan, and MCC's guests trooped off to the Long Room for dinner. There would be more of the same in this festival week. The next night, for instance, Graveney and his wife would be at the Lord's Taverners' annual fundraising dinner.

On the day before the Test, Lord's is hectic. Food and drink arrive in quantities sufficient to satisfy festival appetites. Inexperienced staff are being shown the ropes. The players are practising at the Nursery End, England in the morning and Australia late in the afternoon after a picnic lunch with their wives and families in Regent's Park. Both the captains give press conferences, Vaughan in the film theatre at the back of the Museum. Ponting stands under the trees in the Coronation Garden behind the Warner Stand. That Australia are world champions is obvious from Ponting's ebullient manner. Vaughan, leading a younger team, is conscious of the difficulty of the task ahead.

The Ashes series would be a great test of a young England team, Vaughan said. He admitted that, in the last Ashes series in 2002/03, England might have been 'a bit overawed'. Not any more. 'We'll be taking the game to the Aussies. Our body language is crucial. We're trying to be positive in everything we do.' The difference was that England now had three or four match-winners, and one of them – Andrew Flintoff, was very focused: 'Fred's going to be crucial in the next few weeks.'

Ricky Ponting still had not seen the pitch, and he was anxious to have a look; but the vibrations, he said, were always good at Lord's. Ponting took seriously a suggestion that Australian cricketers feel more at home there than English players. 'Australians love everything about the place,' he said. 'This is like a second home to us. I've never lost a game here, and it is lovely to see Australian names on the boards in the dressing room.' Two honours boards in the visitors' dressing room record every century scored, and every 'five-for' and 'ten-for' taken by visiting players.

An Australian reporter asked whether Ponting would be taking the Ashes urn home this time? 'We've been trying for 20 years,' he said. Even after successive Ashes wins in England, the urn has stayed put in the Museum. The curator said it was too fragile to travel. Since then it has been strengthened and restored, and a trip to Australia is discussed at Lord's, though not as the spoils of any victory in the 2005 series. But Ponting exhibited not a scintilla of doubt about who would hold the Ashes at the end of the series. Only the margin of victory seemed to be in question.

The accent in the ticket office on Wednesday afternoon was Australian. When Simon Wakefield allocated tickets to Australian tour groups, a condition was that members of the group should turn up individually and bring their passports to confirm their identity. 'It did raise a few eyebrows, to be honest,' says Jamie Winton of AST – Australian Sports Tours. But no one objected. 'The Lord's ticket is like a ticket for the Wimbledon final.'

Wakefield did relent, a bit. Tickets for Winton's tour party could be handed over to his assistant, who had brought a large pile of passports. These were checked against the name on the ticket, although these Australians were the people least likely to slip a spare ticket to a tout. Because demand outstripped supply, they had already had to survive the

THE SCORER'S BOX: *'Thursday 23rd June 2005. It's the Middlesex v Surrey Twenty20 Cup – not a cricket white in sight – it's all colour and pop music – heavens above! Crammed into the scorer's box with fans in full flow are Keith Booth, Don Shelley, Brian Rodwell, Charles Fellow-Smith, Dan Kirkpatrick and Andy Scarlett is just out of the picture and about to take the immaculate score book from the table. It's a very jovial atmosphere up here in the scoring epicentre of Lord's.'*

preliminary ordeal of an AST ballot for the 52 tickets allocated each day. Winton took it on himself to phone the unsuccessful applicants, and found it disconcerting. 'One old guy started crying on the phone.'

Now the tour party was in London, being cosseted. On the coach taking them to Lord's each morning, they would get an analysis of the state of play from former England Ashes stalwarts Angus Fraser and Graham Gooch. Specialised tour groups such as this are a recent phenomenon of interna-

tional travel. In 2001, AST brought a group of 90 for the Ashes series. This summer, says Winton, they could have brought a thousand for all the Tests – if they had been able to get the tickets.

The battle with the touts reached a dramatic climax during the night. On Wednesday, Wakefield gathered together a hundred or so tickets that had been recovered from ticket agencies and from people who had been exposed trying to sell their tickets on eBay's auction site. Those tickets would go on sale at 8.30 a.m. the next morning at the North Gate – first come, first served, one ticket per person. The queue formed at midday on Wednesday, headed by a group of Australians with blankets and plenty of grog. By 7 p.m. there were 80 in the queue, which had already disappeared round the corner.

It continued to grow steadily during the night, and it was then that the touts seized their opportunity and queue-barged into promising positions. The police were called. Colin Maynard and Simon Wakefield needed to come up with a counter-strategy – and quick. When the gates opened sharp at 8.30 a.m., those in the queue were not sold a ticket. They bought the right to buy a ticket, and were given bands to wear on their wrists. The ticket would be issued only inside the ground, and, once in, the purchaser would have to stay in. Pass-outs would not be issued, because they could be sold on along with the tickets. There were 30 touts in the queue by the morning, and, when they learned of the restrictions, they melted away, having been out-thought.

THE ASHES TEST

There can be few long queues anywhere to rival the one snaking away from the Grace Gates in terms of prosperity, experience, and longevity. A large number of the men standing obediently in line wear the flamboyant red and yellow – or egg and tomato – MCC tie, rather than the sombre dark-blue version. A handful even drape themselves in egg-and-tomato-coloured blazers. Most are unaccompanied, reading a paper. A few have brought stools or shooting sticks. Straw hats are plentiful.

The morning of 21 July, the first day of the Lord's Test against Australia, was fine and clear, with the promise of warmth in the morning air. MCC members started to queue in the small hours, waiting patiently for the turnstiles at the Grace Gates to open at 8.30 a.m. Two lines stretched away from the Gates. One went west before turning into Grove End Road, with a break in the line for the newspaper stall on the corner, which was doing brisk business in the broadsheet papers. The second went back past the East Gate and the Indoor School.

Only the members waiting in Grove End Road see the third queue that forms outside Lord's on a big match day like this. Catering staff join a line that runs from behind the Tavern Banqueting Suite. There are more than a thousand of them, and they get in sooner than the members do. These are casual workers, hired for the duration of the Test. They are young, scruffily dressed in jeans and sweat-shirts, about to be transformed into smartly uniformed waiters and bar staff. In the passage that leads to the ground

there are clothes rails on which hang rows of freshly laundered shirts in green and blue stripes, and white aprons with 'Lord's' embroidered on the breast. Names are checked off long lists, and the staff are given their lunch – a sandwich, an apple and a small bottle of water. Sometimes an official from the Immigration Service turns up to check visas, but not this morning. Hannah Ray, who manages the Club Facilities Department, and her team are meticulously sellotaping members' names on to the backs of benches in front of the Pavilion. A rectangular section of the seating is set aside for 200 of the over-70s, who must also have completed 25 years of membership. The only way to avoid the queue.

Grant Halstead, who says he arrives each morning at 6.37 precisely, has already made a quick inspection of the Pavilion to check that the first

THE FIRST DAY OF THE ASHES: *'Thursday 21st July 2005 – Finally the big day has arrived and the first test of the Ashes Series gets underway to a capacity audience. And what a whirl-wind of excitement today as balls fly and wickets fall at a great pace – and all over this little terracotta urn. 'The great crowd will feel proud' reads one of the lines on this urn, and they did today as Australia were out for 190 and well, it did look all so promising until the England wickets also continued to fall with great alacrity'.*

cleaning shift – on duty at 5.00 a.m. – has done its job. Like the construction workers in the Pavilion during the winter, the cleaners are mainly from Lithuania. The iceman has come already, leaving plastic sacks of ice piled on pallets, to be distributed round the ground by fork-lift truck. Tables are already being laid for breakfast in Green's Seafood and Oyster Bar in the Harris Garden. Stewards start arriving soon after 7.00 a.m., and line up outside Jeff Cards's office under the Mound Stand. From Cards himself they receive vouchers worth £10 a day which can be redeemed in the Food Village. Stewards clearly rank above waiters. Regulars have their own green blazers; others choose one from clothes rails in the open passageway. Cards is not a stickler for punctuality, but he wants all his stewards in by 8.00 a.m.

Rubbish is being collected in one of the converted milk floats, and at 7.55 a.m. the first of many loads is dumped in the compactor that stands by the turnstiles at the North Gate. Shortly after 8.00 a.m., Alan Pryer, who manages the shop, walks from the accounts department in the Pavilion carrying £2,000 in pound coins in plastic bags – change for the tills. He passes an anonymous-looking small group in white sports shirts and dark trousers. Closer inspection reveals Duncan Fletcher, the England coach, looking unflinchingly ahead of him. Simon Jones, the Welsh swing bowler, looks around him; Ian Bell, the young Warwickshire batsman, acknowledges a mouthed 'good luck' with a nervous smile. Linda Le Ker's kitchen in the players' dining room is already humming, if they feel like a calming cup of tea.

At 8.10 a.m., a burly gateman is yelling crossly at a delivery van driver: 'You're supposed to be off the premises by eight o'clock.' At 8.15 a.m. Johnny Dennis, the PA announcer, tests the microphone. Jim Webb the electrician, holding a neat leather tool case, slips into the back door of the Banqueting Suite. Roger Knight, in a smart light-brown suit, says 'Good Morning' to the jazz band that plays behind the Pavilion. Like many jazz bands, it is made up of good-natured pensioners; at least one of them is an MCC member.

As 8.30 a.m. approaches, the security staff takes up their places at the tables where they will inspect all bags of all spectators, and do a quick body check with a metal detector. Young women stand at the turnstiles, ready to tear off the vouchers for 21 July in the members' passes. A springer spaniel scurries by, led by his minder. This is a sniffer dog, trained to detect explosives. There is a second dog at the North Gates which sniffs around the delivery vans. Only two weeks earlier, 52 men and women had been killed by bombs on the underground and a bus. 'I hope you have a quiet day,' I say. 'You'll soon know if I don't,' replies the minder.

A few reporters wait to watch the 8.30 a.m. scramble as the first members burst through the turnstiles and race towards their chosen seat. The journalists search idly for a metaphor: Running before the bulls in Pamplona? When they do get in, what is striking is the anxiety on their faces. The younger ones dash past older men who do not move so easily anymore. If they are alone, they will mostly make for a seat in the Pavilion – one of the leather chairs in the Writing Room, perhaps. If they have company, the top tier of the Warner Stand is a favourite spot. A few with inside knowledge make for one of the refurbished turrets at each end of the Pavilion.

Only ninety more minutes to go and the captains will be in the middle for the toss, using a George III silver shilling dated 1787 – the year MCC was founded. It was purchased for the occasion by Glenys Williams, the archivist, from Spinks, the coin dealers. The most eagerly awaited Lord's Test for years is to start in two hours.

A remarkably high proportion of the first-day crowd of 30,601 had taken their seats by the time Ricky Ponting won the toss. The blocks of seats for Australians were clearly identifiable by the spectators' yellow-and-green replica shirts and caps. The grass in the Coronation Garden had disappeared almost completely under a patchwork of rugs and picnic baskets – all of which were inspected by a security guard. Anyone who passed the time by scrutinising the scorecard read about England's last win against Australia at Lord's. It was 71 years ago, in 1934, when Hedley Verity, the Yorkshire left-arm spinner, took 8 for 43 in Australia's second innings to give England victory by an innings and 38 runs.

The sky had begun to cloud over. But this was a morning to bat, and Ponting chose to do so. In the first over, Steve Harmison hit Justin Langer a fierce blow on his elbow; soon after Matthew Hayden lost his wicket, Ponting took a fearsome blow on the helmet which opened a bad cut under his right eye. It was as if the crown of a volcano had blown. This was England doing what Vaughan had promised, and taking the game to Australia. When Ponting was cut by the blow, no English player expressed concern. In the President's Box, Tom Graveney was shocked by the violence of the opening round.

Ponting was out soon afterwards, then Damien Martyn. Langer, who knows Lord's intimately from his days as a Middlesex player, stuck around until shortly before lunch. By now the Food Village would normally be crowded with lunchers getting orders in early. But there was hardly a soul to be seen there, and those who stayed in their seats showed sound judgement because Simon Jones had Michael Clarke leg before. Australia were 87 for 5. For the English, at the start of the Ashes series, bliss it was in that dawn to be alive, no matter if you weren't young . . .

The crowd in the Long Room was so deep that Ponting, looking annoyed at his dismissal, had to make his way through a narrow gap between the spectators and the back wall. The Australians had been conscious of the crush, and were fearful that they might be heckled. For the Test match there would be 30 stewards on the doors and entrances to the Pavilion, but they had not been able to make a proper passage for Ponting. The man charged with sorting out the problem was Grant Halstead, the manager in the Pavilion.

Halstead, a Zimbabwean by birth, dresses like the manager of an hotel, which is what he studied to be. His first job at Lord's was as a butler in the MCC Committee box in the Tavern Stand. He is a mild-mannered figure, obliging, as butlers are, but with a streak of the toughness that managers must have. He is deputed to tell members how they must, or must not, behave, which can prove very challenging.

When doormen tell members that they cannot enter the Pavilion wearing jeans, Halstead is called to pacify them. ('But these jeans cost £1,000.' 'Sorry, sir, no jeans.') He can order members to be removed from the Pavilion if they are drunk, or rude to the staff, or ask cricketers for their autographs in the Long Room. No chance of doing that during an Ashes Test, when his principal role is as crowd controller. Even in the new space on the roof, the crowd was three and four deep. The view from high behind the bowler's arm was splendid, except when it was blocked by hats, heads and shoulders.

At the front of the President's Box are three rows of seats open to the air. Sight-lines and angles give you the impression that you are sitting just behind the boundary rope. The view is square of the wicket, but, as Don Bradman said, you can always tell what the ball is doing by watching the players' feet. The guests are pampered. Coffee comes at coffee time, drinks at drinks time – a choice between Pimm's and champagne – and lunch at lunch time, all served by competent and friendly waitresses to whom an empty glass is a dereliction of duty.

At an Ashes Test, the box plays host to past heroes, men who sustained the legend of the Ashes. On the first morning, England was represented by great bowlers – Frank Tyson, John Snow and Trevor Bailey, all of whom had played leading parts in winning Ashes series. From Australia, a trio of the surviving Invincibles from the 1948 touring team were guests in Graveney's box.

Neil Harvey, one of the Invincibles, and Alan Davidson were regular visitors. On the morning of the second day Graveney had more Invincibles, Arthur Morris and Sam Loxton. Morris was a left-handed opening bat in 1948, a burly man who looks younger than his 83 years. Loxton, who is a year older, was not in Morris's class as a player – but Morris was never elected to the Australian Parliament, as Loxton had been.

I mentioned to Graveney that I had seen Morris in 1948. 'So did I,' he replied. 'I was twelfth man in Bristol when he scored 290 against Gloucestershire. Loxton got a big not out hundred, and the Australians scored 774 for 7. It was a slaughter.' Morris's double hundred was his highest score in first-class cricket. I had seen Morris on my tenth birthday in the Fifth Test at the Oval, when his smooth progress towards 196 was interrupted by a brief appearance by Don Bradman, who was bowled second ball by Eric Hollies in his last Test innings. Thus, Bradman's Test average fell below 100 to 99.94.

Morris seemed faintly astonished to receive congratulations on this innings almost 57 years later. Colin McDonald, a mere 76 – the only Australian not to be mesmerised by Jim Laker at Old Trafford in 1956 – and Bobby Simpson were talking to Bob Barber, who scored 185 against Simpson's team in 1965/66. In the context of an Ashes Test at Lord's, the former

Prime Minister Sir John Major seemed a good deal less distinguished than Graveney's Australian visitors.

Because of the spectacular happenings in the middle before lunch, the crowd never thinned. England bowled out Australia, who had batted recklessly, in 40.2 overs. The wicket played well and there did not appear to be anything to stop England getting a decent first-innings lead. Except Glenn McGrath. When Justin Langer caught Marcus Trescothick for 4, McGrath celebrated his 500th Test wicket. In less than an hour, England's position shifted violently from promising to disastrous. Five wickets were lost for 21 runs, all of them to McGrath, who was using the seam, and bowling just outside the off stump with the accuracy and consistency of a metronome, taking advantage of the Lord's slope. Bowling from the Pavilion End, the slope sometimes exaggerates his inswing. McGrath bowled Vaughan, Bell and Flintoff for fewer than 10 runs between them.

Glenn McGrath of Australia holds the ball with which he took his 500th Test wicket. McGrath's victim was Marcus Trescothick, caught by Langer for 4, on the first day of the first Test at Lord's. The ball and McGrath's golden boots are now in the Lord's Museum.

By the close, England were 98 runs behind Australia with three wickets standing; seventeen wickets had fallen in a day. If it were a county game, the ECB pitch inspectors would been called in to have a look. Some thought the delivery that bowled Vaughan had kept low, until a TV replay showed that the ball hit the top quarter of the stump. The ball was swinging readily, but bowlers always hope it will on the first day of a Lord's Test. Questions about the wicket probably had more to do with the search for an excuse for England's feeble batting. Whatever the motive, this was a debate in which Mick Hunt did not intend to participate.

In mid-morning on the second day of the Test, Jim Webb, the electrician, was sitting in his workshop drinking a cup of milky coffee and watching the cricket – which was being played not 25 yards away – on a fuzzy TV. There's nothing he can do about the reception. He gets two tickets for two of the first four days in the staff section of the Compton Lower Stand, but this was not one of those days. He noted, however, that heads of department do rather better – two tickets for each of the first four days.

He had been doing the rounds since 7.00 a.m., checking cables in the Food Village, and doing odd jobs in the Pavilion and the Banqueting Suite. The big news of the day was a disaster in the Pavilion in the small hours. A pipe connecting the washing machine in the players' dining room kitchen had come apart, and the powerful water supply poured out onto the floor of the kitchen for a long time. The players' dining room is at the back of the second floor, and the water had gushed down through the ceiling on the first floor and on down to the Old Library on the ground floor, bringing down a chandelier and spoiling furniture and carpets. A major clean-up had begun first thing in the morning. Fortunately, the fault lay not with Jim's mate Ron the plumber, but with the contractors who had rebuilt all the electrical and plumbing services in the Pavilion during the winter.

Webb was downstairs. Upstairs, in the President's Box, Graveney was standing at the back of the seats and watching a minor England revival, led by their debutant, Kevin Pietersen. He was astonished by Martyn's diving catch on the boundary to dismiss Pietersen. But Pietersen had already used his powerful forearms and sinewy wrists to hit Shane Warne for six just below the President's Box. Better still, he had hit McGrath straight into the Pavilion. His 57 was a remarkable first Test innings, Graveney said. Effective biffing by Simon Jones contributed 20 to a last-wicket stand of 33. England were 35 runs behind – not as bad as they must have feared.

Paul Dumpleton is called an events safety officer. It means that he is in charge of security at Lord's, and he was acutely conscious of the terrorist threat. 'At the moment, there's nothing else in the sports world to compete with this Test. The hype! It's *the* target,' he said. Roger Knight had reassured the Australians after the London bombings on 7 July. His message was that, without being blasé, they felt they had got security almost as right as they could; the subtext was that, ultimately, no public place like Lord's can be 100 per cent safe. After discussion with the police and the ECB, security was made even tighter for this Test.

The second wave of bombs in London occurred on the first day of the Test. The coach due to take the Australian players' wives and girlfriends back to their hotel was caught up in the traffic chaos. MCC brought them and their children into the Committee Room to wait for the players and take the team coach.

Although none of the bombs had exploded and no one had been killed, the biggest manhunt in the history of the Metropolitan Police was under way. The Australians asked MCC for further reassurance. John Buchanan, the coach, had reported to MCC that players were worried about the safety of their wives. Dumpleton had promised that the police would talk to them.

Even before the bombs, the Australians were concerned about player protection, outside the Long Room as well as inside. 'It's a big issue with them,' said Dumpleton. 'We have to keep them up to date.' In the Long Room, Halstead had roped off a passageway through the crowd. On the ground, Dumpleton told the stewards who sit sideways on to the pitch on the perimeter of the playing area to stand between overs to remind the crowd that they were there. But the most effective safeguards are the bag searches and metal detectors at the entrance gates. 'That's what a terrorist would notice.'

The sniffer dogs are a second line of defence. I mentioned to Dumpleton that the keeper of the springer spaniel by the Grace Gates had said that the dogs were trained to detect only metallic objects, and not drugs. 'I don't know about that,' he said. 'We put one on the West Indies' team coach a few years back, and it went mad.'

On the second day of the Test, Dumpleton had an additional concern. John Howard, Australia's cricket-mad Prime Minister and an MCC member, who had some urgent business in London that happened to coincide with the Lord's Test, was due to visit. 'He's a terrorist target, so plenty of care had to be taken,' said Dumpleton. On Friday afternoon, a procession of long black cars with their motor-cycle outriders pulled up in the lee of the Grand Stand so that the Prime Minister might enjoy a little rest and recreation. He was ushered from his car to the President's Box without lingering in public.

Dumpleton sits at a long desk, flanked by two ambulance controllers, a radio controller and MCC's head of security, Alan Baxter. The police sit in a second row of seats. They are there to assist Dumpleton's operation, though, if there were a major event such as a bomb, the Met would take control. Above them is a row of screens divided into 20 separate panels, which can show pictures from the 132 CCTV cameras on the ground. Five Live's commentary is playing, as is Channel 4's TV coverage. In the clutter surrounding Dumpleton, there is a laptop and a printer, a telephone, two walkie-talkies, and a powerful pair of binoculars. A light breeze comes in through the open window, along with a buzz from the crowd.

The job of an events security officer is a new one, created after the Hillsborough disaster in 1989, when 96 people died, and the police were heavily criticised. The occupation has now been legitimised by a series of examinations, which Dumpleton has passed, at all levels. He is a burly man, a former superintendent in the Hertfordshire police, who learned his trade running security at Watford Football Club. Now he concentrates on major matches at Lord's, making sure that the ground complies with the safety certificate issued by Westminster Council. (A council inspector has to attend every big game – the poor thing.)

Most of the work is either routine or mundane. Stewards report pathways that have become slippery with spilled beer and need to be washed down; metal barriers are configured so as to create the easiest routes out of the ground. MCC catering staff report the unexplained presence of a green vehicle. A black bag lies unattended in the Food Village: a policeman goes to investigate, but it has gone by the time he gets there. The Burger Bar in the Food Village is doing the washing-up in a place that might impede emergency medical access. St John Ambulance men seem to spend a great deal of time sitting around, but that day they had had work to do. A major medical emergency had occurred in the Tavern Stand at 9.30 a.m. on the first day, and on the second morning a man had collapsed in the members' queue.

At 5.00 p.m., all the public bars close, and Dumbleton checks via his camera pictures that the process takes place in an orderly manner. Soon afterwards, John Howard's motor-cycle escort revs up, and he is driven off. At a tense time in London, it has been a quiet shift.

Johnny Dennis, the public-address announcer, does not bother to say how a batsman has been dismissed. The crowd can watch it happen on the replay screen, and get the details from the scoreboards. He concentrates on half-centuries and centuries, and on bowling changes. Short, neat, always properly dressed, Dennis is a familiar voice but an anonymous figure at England's Tests. He aims to say as little as possible, and in the second session, after lunch on the second day of the Test, there was little for him to say.

Australia were batting again, and their third wicket had fallen at 100. Quick wickets now, and England would have a chance. Michael Clarke, the team's only young batsman, came out to join Damien Martyn, and England's bowlers would have fancied their chances against him. Before the Test, Clarke was badly out of form and he had scored only 11 in the first innings. England got their chance, too, but Pietersen dropped Clarke at short extra cover on 21, just before tea.

Dennis had nothing to say until Clarke reached 50, and then Martyn followed suit. He waits until the end of the over. 'If there is applause, you let it run. You don't interrupt and cause a dying fall.' If he can, he will make his announcement before the applause builds, which builds it further. 'It's a theatrical thing,' he says. He adds a deliberate pause when he is announcing a bowling change, to try to create a little drama. Dennis is an actor.

The hundred partnership came up, and then 150. As I sat with Dennis, we could feel the match slipping away from England. Then a flurry of wickets revived England's hopes. On 255, Clarke was bowled just 9 runs short of a hundred in his first Lord's Test. He and Martyn had put on 155 together in 208 balls, and Australia were now 290 ahead. But Martyn was out for 67 with the score still on 255. Two more wickets fell before the close, including that of the fearsome Adam Gilchrist. The lead was 314. England would have to take three wickets very cheaply indeed the following morning to have any hope.

Dennis's workplace is a cubicle six feet square, next to the match referee and the third and fourth umpires at the top of the Warner Stand. He misses his box in the Pavilion, which was behind the bowler's arm. Since he is unable to see either scoreboard, a screen tells him the score on his desktop. A second screen relays the TV coverage. Sound bounces off the buildings that enclose the ground at Lord's, which means a closed window, to prevent his announcements feeding back into his microphone. 'I don't feel quite in the game here,' he says.

Dennis has been announcing at cricket matches since the 1970s, when his friend Brian Johnston suggested he would be a capable stand-in, if necessary, for another actor named Alan Curtis. When Curtis fell ill ten years ago, Dennis was taken on full-time by the ECB for whole Test series. By 2004, he had clocked up a hundred Tests and around two hundred one-day internationals.

On stage, he worked regularly with the farceur, Brian Rix. He played the Porter to Michael Gambon's Macbeth, in Billingham of all places, and was Grumio to Joss Ackland's Petruchio in *The Taming of the Shrew*. 'I always intended to play the clown,' he says. He still takes stage and TV jobs when he gets them. Test cricket is a change of pace for him.

Dennis is particularly fond of Lord's. 'The food is brilliant, best on the circuit,' he says. It takes him three and a half minutes precisely to get from his box to the players' dining room, where he eats. Since he has to be back in his seat before the bell rings to announce the return of the umpires, he cannot dawdle, especially during the 20-minute tea interval. He does not mind the dash. The food is worth it.

MCC Young Cricketers have no fixture during the Lord's Test. They have work to do. Clive Radley organises the schedule. Bowlers will be in the nets, doing their best to dismiss one of the English or Australian batsmen who turn up for a practice knock before play starts. A small crew will help the ground staff, guiding the long hovercraft cover towards the middle where it protects the pitch at close of play, and when bad weather threatens. They have had it easy for the first three days of the Test, which have been free of interruptions.

The hardest work is done by the Young Cricketers helping out in the shop, which has its busiest days of the year during the Test. Turnover was more than £100,000 on each of the first two days, and by the fourth day much of the stock was sold out. Business this year was up 50 per cent on the best-ever days: 'Better than we could ever have hoped for,' says Alan Pryer, the shop's manager. The place was like a madhouse, and extra hands were manna from heaven. Not all the Young Cricketers felt they were doing something useful, however, regarding experience in the retail trade as unworthy of their talent. Pryer complained to Clive Radley about the truculent manner of one Young Cricketer, who would clearly have preferred to be with the ground staff. Radley sent him back to do another shift in the shop.

Linda Le Ker, the chef, invited me for a bacon roll in the players' dining room on the morning of the third day. The bread was light, the bacon tasty. For me, it confirmed her reputation. Fred Flintoff calls it the best restaurant in London. 'Bless him,' she says. Le Ker is small, and plump, with a fabulous head of black and silver hair, and a big, easy smile. She looks spotless in her white chef's coat.

No expense is spared in her kitchen. Le Ker reports that Roger Knight always says the players come first. Virtually all the food is delivered fresh each morning by the butcher, the fishmonger and the greengrocer. Though she does concede that you can get away with frozen peas.

The menu board still showed the previous day's menu: vegetable soup, chicken breast with white wine and tarragon, baked cod fillet with leek and prawns and vegetable pasta. Visiting teams do not take chances, however. Diet sheets arrive in advance. Much of the advice is gratuitous – no fried food, no batter, everything steamed, semi-skimmed milk, and fromage frais for cooking, not, God forbid, cream. 'It's what I've been giving them, anyway,' she says.

Since the ingredients must be easily digested, soup is a speciality of the house. Fresh every day – leek and potato, carrot and coriander, squash and sweet potato. The only commonplace item you will not find on the menu is duck. Mike Gatting, the dining room's most loyal customer, said duck sent the wrong message. (But Gatting is a batsman. Why should bowlers not eat duck?)

Linda Le Ker serves the tastiest bacon roll in England and much more besides.

Cricketers do not eat less than they did when Le Ker was given the job of catering manageress, eventually succeeding a strong-minded Irish woman called Nancy Doyle who had little time for fancy vegetables or diet sheets. When Mike Brearley, the celebrated captain of Middlesex as well as England, suggested modifications to the menu, Nancy's response was: 'Mike, I won't tell you how to f***ing bat if you don't tell me how to f***ing cook.'

'But they do eat differently,' says Le Ker. 'When I came here, there was hardly any fish, and they never used to eat salad, never touched it. It was mainly chips, as well. Now it is little boiled new potatoes.' Flintoff had a big appetite for sausages, but not any more: 'He'll eat a rib-eye steak, but no chips. He just has vegetables. He always has dessert, but they need a sugar intake you know.'

The exception to this rule is Shane Warne. 'He always has toasted cheese sandwiches, cheddar cheese, which he eats during the day.' At close of play, Le Ker's kitchen provides the dressing rooms with thin-crust pizza, chicken kebabs and Mediterranean prawns. There is a toaster in the visitors' dressing room, in case Warne wants another cheese sandwich. 'There's never been a request that's not been fulfilled.'

The raw materials are delivered before Le Ker arrives at 7.00 a.m. Three people work in the small kitchen that lies between the players' and the committee dining rooms, which Le Ker also caters for. She does 150–160 covers every lunch time, two sittings for the players, their entourages, and the umpires. 'They're all hungry, and they want it now. But you've got to serve the umpires first because they're the first back on the field. Woe betide any of the girls who forget the umpires.' When they have finished, she feeds the MCC staff. There is hardly anything left over.

Le Ker is not a professional restaurateur. She and her husband Alain – who buys wine for MCC – ran a pub in Camden Town: 'We were very foodie; ahead of our time.' She has strong opinions, and is not afraid to voice them. She is friendly with Justin Langer and John Buchanan, from their Middlesex days – happy days for Langer; frustrating for Buchanan, who was sacked. 'I said my piece at the time. I'm so glad he fell on his feet.'

On Saturday morning, Brett Lee was soon out; Australia were 289 for 8. Then England succumbed. Perhaps it was the pressure of a Lord's Test, or the frustration at expectations unfulfilled, but this was like the worst of times in the 1990s. Bowlers got the length wrong, catches were dropped, the wicketkeeper lost it. Two Australian tailenders, guided by Simon Katich, put on 95 more runs. I consulted the oracle. 'England produced the most ridiculous fielding lapses you've ever seen. It was a shambles,' said Richie Benaud.

Benaud left Channel 4's commentary box in the Media Centre to chat to me about Lord's. His first Test match game on the ground was 52 years ago, in the legendary 1953 series that also saw Tom Graveney's first Ashes Test at Lord's. The stubborn stand between Willie Watson and Trevor Bailey, batting through most of the last day, then won an unlikely draw, and that made it possible for England to regain the Ashes at the Oval. Neither Graveney nor Benaud performed memorably, but Benaud remembers his first visit to the ground. It was the day after the boat docked at Tilbury. At breakfast in their London hotel, Neil Harvey said that they were going to Lord's. Benaud said he hadn't finished unpacking, but Harvey said he was going anyway. When they arrived in front of Lord's Tavern, Harvey told them to be still, keep quiet, and sense the aura. Benaud, still just a boy from Paramatta, was unmoved. Already exhibiting the laconic turn of phrase that graces his TV commentary, he pointed out that Lord's wasn't flat. 'Jeezzz, Harv, it slopes.' Not to be out-done, Harvey replied, 'It slopes. So would you if you were 139 years old!'

Benaud played in two more series, though only one more Test at Lord's. He was injured in 1961. 'I didn't do anything at Lord's that year except be nervous and watch Neil Harvey, who had taken over as captain and won the game.' But he had left his mark in 1957. Keith Miller took ten wickets, but it was, he says, a pretty good match for him too. 'I caught Colin Cowdrey in the gully, took a couple of wickets, including Peter May with a top-spinner, and scored a very quick 97, most of them before lunch on the fourth morning.' Perhaps only Graveney can rival his attendance record at Lord's.

Including his three series as a player, the summer of 2005 was the 15th Ashes series Benaud had watched in England. When he became a journalist, his first Test at Lord's in 1963 was one of the best. Cowdrey saved England from defeat by the West Indies when he came out as last man to bat with a broken arm in plaster. He did not have to face though, as David Allen blocked out Wes Hall's last two balls, when England needed only 6 to win.

Benaud was interrupted by the approach of John Howard, who wanted to shake his hand. 'Sorry to interrupt. Good to see you. Interesting game,' said the Prime Minister. 'As good as you get,' replied Benaud. Howard went on his way as Benaud elaborated. 'The first and second days and the third morning were quite extraordinary. This is one of the most amazing matches I've seen, and it's not half over yet.'

Would this be his last commentary at Lord's? 'Who knows? I might drop off the twig tomorrow. So might you.' Enough talk about mortality. Does he still feel the aura? 'They've done so much in recent years. It was an old traditional ground. Now it's a new traditional ground. The things they've done in recent years are absolutely magnificent. The new Grand Stand, the roof of the Pavilion, the Mound Stand I love. And this is a terrific Media Centre.' Not everything was perfectly fine however. 'The TV commentary box was designed by someone who may or may not have been to a cricket match, but who knows nothing about television.'

Shane Warne had just begun a mesmerising spell of spin bowling in which he dismissed three of England's top six batsmen, and erased any possibility of an England win. Watching him, Benaud said: 'I sometimes think Australians feel more at home at Lord's than English people do.'

In the President's Box, Tom Graveney considered Vaughan's technique. He had been bowled for 4 by Brett Lee after having been bowled by McGrath for 3 in the first innings. 'The bat is not coming down straight,' he said, and Australia's fast bowlers were able to exploit a gap between bat and pad. He feared that Vaughan's hundreds in Australia during the last tour there might prove to be the high point of his batting for England. He had reservations about Geraint Jones behind the wicket, too.

John Howard, his distinguished guest, would have had the opportunity to meet some old English heroes rather than the Australian ones. Ray Illingworth and John Edrich had brought their wives. Derek Underwood looked cheerful. Graveney's brother Ken had arrived from the United States. The old professionals were not entirely approving of the behaviour of their successors. Graveney is rarely judgemental, but he had harsh words about the behaviour of Duncan Fletcher and his charges, the evening before, at MCC Committee's drinks party for the players, which is a fixture on Friday evening of every Test.

At that party, Graveney made sure that the survivors of the Invincibles were present – Morris, Harvey and Loxton. The Australian team members, who had originally said that they would not attend, did appear and stayed to chat, having more reverence for famous old players than England's cricketers. Graveney described them marching in behind Fletcher, and then marching out again, barely stopping to say hello.

Between 6.30 p.m. and 7.00 p.m., when the crowd is streaming through the North Gate on the way to the underground, 150 men and women in blue shorts walk in the opposite direction, making for a shed on the edge of the Nursery Ground. Their names are ticked off on a list, and they come away with brushes of various sizes and big shovels. Walking towards the public stands, they chatter to each other. 'It's Portuguese. They all come from Brazil,' says Chris Economou, an Australian Greek-Cypriot who runs a cleaning company called Tower Group Services. This specialises in sporting venues such as Lord's, and cleans everything except the Pavilion and the private boxes, which are taken care of by MCC cleaners.

Economou's speciality is finding cohesive groups of cleaners from South America. His company had cleaned the Oval for years with Ecuadorians and Colombians, but that ended in grief for the Ecuadorians: the two groups did not get on. When the company got the contract at Lord's, the crew were Ecuadorians and Brazilians, but they did not get on, either. 'I went the Brazilian way,' he says.

He insists that everyone has a national insurance number, a visa, and a passport. 'I'm not taking any chances.' Though he does not need to in the case of a number of Brazilians who have acquired EU passports from Italy, Spain and Portugal. 'There's a community of Brazilians,' he says. 'It's who they know. It's relatives. Lots are young students. Others have jobs in restaurants, and take days off from their regular jobs. Luckily, they do what I ask them to do, and they have fun doing it.' They get fourteen days' work a summer, for which they are paid £5.50 an hour. They are the neat successors to the motley crew of homeless men and alcoholics who once did the job.

Three shifts work from 7.00 a.m. until 11.00 p.m., but the biggest in terms of manpower is the evening shift that goes through the filthy and cluttered stands. First they pick up bottles and packaging, shovelling it all into black bin bags. Next the sweepers come through, before the small brushes pick up small items such as cigarette butts. The job takes about two and a half hours on a dry day, longer when it has been wet. Another team arrives at 7.00 a.m. to tidy up anything left over from the night before. An hour later, the lavatory-cleaning squad comes on duty, and stays till the close of play. Some hardy souls work a double shift of fourteen hours. It is not unusual, in London now, that the dirty work is done, automatically, by foreigners.

On the fourth day, rain prevents play starting at 10.30 a.m., as scheduled. Heavy overnight rain has turned to drizzle, but it hardly matters. England's condition at the close – five wickets had fallen for 156 – meant there was no great urgency for the start. The game cannot last much longer. Plenty of time for a leisurely breakfast.

Hungry MCC members in the early-morning queue need not wait long. Cooks in the kitchen on the first floor of the Tavern Banqueting Suite are put up in local hotels so that they can be on duty at 4.00 a.m. They have no fewer than 2,000 breakfasts to prepare: 400 to 500 will be consumed in the Banqueting Suite, and the rest sent round the ground in the form of bacon rolls. Bacon has become the food of choice for a morning at the cricket. There are trays of it, ready for imminent despatch.

A meat tray contains five fine fillets of beef, ready for roasting. These will be carved in the bar behind the Long Room. The first stage of a pudding is begun with a layer of tangerines. Fish comes up from the storage fridges downstairs. No chef raises his or her voice. There is no occasion to. The atmosphere may well get more heated as lunch approaches, but the main kitchen at breakfast time is an orderly place.

Michael Parkinson was hosting a box in the Tavern Stand for all four days of the Test. He has been MCC's most caustic critic for more than 40 years, but, when he was asked how he would prefer to celebrate his 70th birthday, he said he could think of nothing finer than the Ashes Test. Damn the expense. A friend organised the box for him. Parkinson is not, never has been, and never will be an MCC member.

Parkinson has been MCC's greatest irritant. A Yorkshireman who opened the innings for Barnsley with Dickie Bird, the umpire, he was probably born with Lord's in his sights. He would have learned at his father's knee that MCC was southern, toffee-nosed, and reactionary. When he grew up, he hated the idea of cricket being run by 'Gubby' Allen, in collaboration with E. W. Swanton of the *Daily Telegraph* (Parkinson worked for the *Guardian* at the time).

His friends in cricket were anti-establishmentarian Australians such as Bill O'Reilly and Jack Fingleton, whom he got to know when he was an outspoken journalist on the *Sunday Times*. He never minded the fact that his great heroes – led by F. S. Trueman – were delighted to become honorary life members of MCC, but he never wanted to join them.

Why is he there, then? 'Because it's a great place to watch cricket.' He points across to the Grand Stand, and then to the Edrich and Compton Stands before looking to the Mound Stand. 'Say no more,' he says. You do not have to admire MCC to love Lord's.

The rain stopped, the sky cleared, and the surface water drained away in the sandy soil of the newly laid outfield. Play started at 3.45 p.m., and ended not too long after. England's last five wickets fell for 24 runs, four of them for nine runs in five overs, before Kevin Pietersen hit out and took his score to 64 not out. Australia had won the Lord's Test at a canter, by 239 runs.

Four of the five wickets had fallen to Glenn McGrath, who took his match figures to 9 for 82.

It was a dismal end for England, and a triumph for McGrath, who was the only serious candidate for Man of the Match. 'I love bowling here,' he said afterwards. 'I think the slope helps, and to get my 500th wicket here …' Words failed him. In anticipation, his boot suppliers had made a special pair, decorated with gold panels. McGrath privately and quietly presented them as a short-term loan to the Lord's Museum. Australian players began to talk about taking the series 5 to 0, and while some were playing mind games, McGrath, for one, believed it.

Michael Vaughan was despondent. What else? 'We didn't handle the pressure the way they did,' he said. He thought England were level pegging when Australia's lead was 165 with three down in their second innings. 'We wanted a chance to chase 250 to 270. We had an opportunity, and we didn't take it. What you can't do with good sides is give them a second chance,' he said.

Like a good captain, Vaughan asked for tolerance from fans and cricket writers, not vituperation. 'This is a young set of players. Give them a chance.' As the rest of the series was to show, given the chance, they were capable of taking it.

At his press conference, Vaughan was asked whether the English authorities had blundered in scheduling the First Test for Lord's instead of Edgbaston, where England regularly win Tests. Vaughan was emphatic: No mistake had been made. Others thought differently. By starting at Lord's, they felt, England had shot themselves in the foot.

Why do England lose at Lord's? Amend that to 'usually lose', because in the first five years of the twenty-first century they have beaten the West Indies, New Zealand, India, Pakistan, Zimbabwe and Bangladesh at Lord's, winning eight of the twelve Tests played since the summer of 1999 – the nadir of modern English cricket, when New Zealand won by nine wickets. They have not beaten South Africa or Sri Lanka, but what we are really talking about is the way they always choke against Australia.

Watching from her kitchen, Linda Le Ker has an idea why it is that the Australians always do well at Lord's and England do not. 'For them, it's history, hallowed turf. You see it when they come up here. They enjoy it from the start. The English are just not impressed by it.'

Mike Gatting knows the ground, and the opponents, and the answer. 'Since it's the ground that everyone wants to play on, visiting teams are all switched on. They know they might have only one chance to play there, and they know if they can get their name on the board in the visitors' dressing room, they'll be famous. They focus that much more. I suppose that's why England feel under more pressure.' England left Lord's under a cloud.

That evening the victorious Australians stayed in their dressing room for hours, savouring their moment, and Linda Le Ker's snacks. Shane Warne and Simon Katich snaffled large helpings of pizzas. The leg-spinner, Stuart MacGill, kept the drink flowing. That night, Lord's – their second home – belonged to them.

FOLLOW THE MONEY

Simon Gibb was shocked when he arrived at Lord's in 2001 to take up the position of club accountant. He had come from Whitbread, once brewers, now big players in the hospitality industry. There, he took for granted efficient financial accounting methods based on sophisticated IT systems. But there were very few computer screens in the Lord's accounts department for the simple reason that there was no sophisticated IT system. He felt as if he had gone back a hundred years in a time machine. Clerks did not sit at high stools, quite, but some of the accounts were still kept in large leather-bound books, with titles in gold leaf. Bills were written on the single office typewriter, and many staff wages were paid weekly, in cash. 'It was a nightmare,' says Gibb.

Nosing about the departmental storeroom, he discovered the *draft* accounts for the 1981 Benson and Hedges cup final. Gibb is keen on a good archive, but this seemed over the top. A set of large brass scales was used to count the coins as they came in. When he asked for financial information on a spreadsheet, the office staff was perplexed.

His department was not instinctively sympathetic to newcomers. There was a pervasive feeling of 'them and us' that meant that the workers liked to believe that, while they laboured in the damp basement of the Pavilion, their leaders were enjoying a gin and tonic in the Committee Room before going upstairs to the dining room for a long lunch. There might have been something in that: food and drink were a perk of power at a members' club. Cultural diversity was unheard of. Interdepartmental rivalry bred deeper discontent.

The accounts department is now in the refurbished Pavilion basement. In a corner office, Gibb has a good view of the members' feet as they pass by. The staff must find it difficult to explain to outsiders that working in a cricket ground does not mean they get a view, and that they have to follow a game on TV. The room is now lit partly by computer screens. Gibb's first task has been to produce his 'IT vision'. With help from KPMG, they produced a comprehensive solution. But the proposed cost was in the region of £200,000.

Before Gibb presented the proposal to the finance committee, he was nervous. He had no idea what the reaction would be, but he believed a principle was involved. If MCC did not want his system, he did not want to work at Lord's. But it would be a pity to leave after only six months. As with other recent recruits with a commercial approach, the romance of cricket had been a powerful motive for taking a job at Lord's. As a boy Gibb had represented Reading Schools, and he had gone on to play competitive club cricket. Now he likes to turn out for Cross Arrows on the Nursery Ground in September, and to play some village cricket. He need not have worried about his proposals. The finance committee was enthusiastic, and he was told to go ahead.

It is not correct, however, to see Gibb as an unrepentant capitalist. He is conscious of the limits to commerce at a club like MCC. As an example, he tells a story about ticket prices for the Ashes Test. The Oval had announced a top price of £66 for the Fifth Test. Should MCC follow suit? There was no question that they could have sold out at £66 – they could charge £100 and still fill the house. But £66 tickets would create substantial windfall profits, and these would be interpreted by MCC's critics as profiteering. That would be bad publicity. The MCC Committee decided that £58 was enough. In a members' club that makes a comfortable financial surplus, it would be hard to argue against this. Gibb makes the case admirably, but you can sense the small part of him that thinks profit is there to be maximised.

Gibb's principal business is not public relations or corporate governance. He is the man with the figures at his fingertips. He knows about the wall of money that hits Lord's on New Year's Day, when members pay their subscription by direct debit. Of a total subscription base of £4.5m, MCC banks £4m on 1 January. About £200,000 is rejected by members' bankers because their banking details change. Some full members live unwisely and too well over Christmas, and thus lack the funds in their account to meet the bill of £324.

The decision to put tickets on sale earlier in the winter – two Tests the following summer required a larger sales window – means that, come the New Year, a further £2m has already been paid for tickets for the coming summer's Tests. Gibb does not let these millions lie in the bank. MCC has two accounts in the London money market, in one-month and three-month money accounts that earn interest roughly equivalent to the Bank of England's base rate. Net interest in 2004 was £248,000.

By March, more ticket money is banked, along with the cash from the hire of 70 boxes, either permanently, for the whole season, or to individuals for single days in a Test. All this money, plus interest, provides Lord's with enough cash until the end of November, when it starts to run out. But they have only one month to wait before the millions flow again.

Gibb and Oliver Stocken, the Treasurer, have recently begun to reduce costs by taking advantage of a clever piece of financial engineering. A layman will find the details forbidding, but what it means is that MCC uses interest earned on their current accounts at Barclays, MCC's bankers, to offset the rate of interest paid on outstanding loans – in this case, the £1.8m borrowed to build the Grand Stand. This is called an offset agreement. Since Barclays do not do as well out of this deal as MCC, they did not offer it out of the goodness of their heart. NatWest, which was anxious to poach MCC's business, offered something similar, and Barclays valued the account sufficiently to match the offer.

To find out how much money cricket earns at Lord's, you must turn to MCC's annual report, which contains detailed figures for Tests and one-day internationals in 2004. That was a bumper year for Lord's, with Tests against New Zealand and the West Indies lasting well into the fifth day, plus a couple of extra one-day internationals at the end of the season. Ticket sales produced a record income of £8,590,000.

MCC's income from Tests comes from a staging fee, which in 2004 was £2,307,000. On top of that, there is a commission on ticket sales (£1,100,000), and a payment from a seating scheme that is intended to encourage Test grounds to put more bums on seats. Since Lord's has increased its capacity, and particularly its good seats, it gets more money from the seating scheme than the other Test grounds. It amounted to £1,157,000 in 2004. This all adds up to £4,564,000. Deducted from net sales (£6,785,000), it provided the ECB with revenue from international cricket at Lord's of £2,221,000 – more than twice as much as in 2003.

Despite the presence of the Australians, the 2005 season was not as productive. For a start, there was significantly less Test cricket: England lasted only four days in the Ashes Test, and Bangladesh were swept away by England before lunch on the third day. The staging agreement produces much the same revenue (£2.4m) no matter how many days are played, but fewer bums on seats means that the income from commissions on ticket sales (£899,000) and the seat scheme (£850,000) would be down on 2004.

In the Ashes Test, the benefits of David Batts's ebullient commercialism began to appear on the balance sheet. Taking catering in-house led to a substantial increase in spending – on wages, raw materials and new facilities. A robust attitude was taken to this: the chef was told: 'You've been moaning and groaning about your kitchen. Now you've got new kit, we want better quality from your kitchen, and fewer people running round like headless chickens.' Sodexho, the contract caterers, had paid MCC £1m a year. 'The first target was to make sure we didn't make any less,' says Gibb.

The Ashes Test was good news. The presence of the Australians is excellent for advertising. The boards round the ground are expected to bring in £1m in 2005, most of it profit. Tours were expected to attract more than 30,000 visitors through the year, and show a profit of £45,000. At the end of the Ashes series, the marketing department reported a gratifying increase in business reservations for dinners, conferences and parties. Revenue from the Indoor School – it is also a gym – was £350,000.

On the other side of the income and expenditure account, Lord's spends £6m on wages and salaries to 160 permanent staff, and to as many as 1,800 casual workers on big match days. Cash in brown envelopes is a thing of the past. Apart from two employees who cannot, for the life of them, open a bank account, everyone gets paid monthly, directly to their bank account.

The one area that remains untouched by Batts's commercial drive is, of course, cricket. More than £1m is spent on Mick Hunt, his groundsmen and the ground, and on Clive Radley's cricket staff, including the MCC Young Cricketers, and on match expenses. Over £650,000 is handed out in grants to cricket at home and overseas, and that sum will rise sharply in 2005, when MCC universities receive a grant of £400,000.

The bottom line? MCC's income is greater than its expenditure – Mr Micawber's recipe for happiness. At a big match, when things are humming, Gibb notices that the buzz cheers the accounts staff in their basement hide-away. He also reports that a survey in 2004 asked members of the crowd to rate their day, from disappointing to fantastic; '98 per cent said fantastic.' He was, he says, a bit disappointed: 'If they're all happy, what do you work on next?'

Gibb will no doubt find new schemes to play with. He is now toying with the efficiencies to be derived from replacing barmen in private boxes with an electronic ordering system that would serve drinks from a central bar. He is not thinking entirely of the income and expenditure account. If only one large tot of whisky is poured from a bottle at the bar, the box-holder pays £40 for the whole bottle: 'Not good for customer relations,' says the accountant.

CATCHING THEM YOUNG

Tom Graveney lives in Cheltenham. Together we went to the cricket ground at Cheltenham College, which is a few hundred yards down the road from the brick house behind a high wall where he has lived for thirteen years. MCC Young Cricketers were playing Gloucestershire's 2nd XI, and Graveney was recognised soon after he entered the ground. 'How's the MCC?' he was asked. 'It's woken me up,' he replied.

On a grey day, the outline of the Cotswold Hills was barely visible. Clive Radley, the Young Cricketers' coach, reported to Graveney that the team were playing well against county second teams, such as this one, even though it was bolstered by Martyn Ball, the off-spinner and England's brilliant specialist substitute fielder on their last tour of India.

They had received a harsh introduction to cricket at this level by Yorkshire IIs in their first game in the 2nd XI Championship. Not putting a fine point on it, Radley said they had been stuffed by a team that included two former Test players, Chris Silverwood and Richard Blakey. The game went from bad to worse when a nasty eye injury to the promising Danish wicketkeeper Freddie Klokker put him in hospital. Three weeks later, Radley was still not sure whether Klokker would lose the sight of an eye. But he had made a full recovery and was batting when Graveney arrived.

Klokker's accident had been in April, only four weeks after the season had begun. Since then the team had drawn with Surrey IIs, lost to Loughborough UCCE, the strongest of the university teams, and beaten both Cambridge and Oxford UCCEs in one-day games. The Oxford game had been remarkable for

205

THE NURSERY GROUND: '*Wednesday 24th August 2005 – Baaaaah humbug! It's not all fun and sun in the world of cricket. Today through the rain and the leaden skies, resigned faces and hands in pockets amidst an array of colourful umbrellas – it definitely seems that rain has stopped play (from even starting) for Thirsk and West Meon & Warnford cricket clubs playing the Thomas Lord 250th Anniversary Match here on the Nursery Ground… where's the tea and beer stand?*'

a performance by Robin Marlar, MCC's President-designate. Marlar, who is MCC's official mentor at Oxford UCCE, is intolerant of shouting by fieldsmen, no matter whether it is abuse or encouragement.

Oxford's players were making a lot of noise, and Marlar suggested to Oxford's coach that he should go out to the middle and tell them to shut up. The coach said that he would pass on the message at lunchtime. That was not good enough for Marlar, who is not a man to stand idly by. He walked

up to the Oxford captain in the middle and asked him to call his team together, and told them how they ought to behave. After he returned to the boundary, the noise level fell sharply. Graveney agreed with the sentiment, but was astonished at Marlar's pro-active method. His successor's term promised more incidents than his own, which had taken a smooth and dignified course.

At Cheltenham, MCC were off to a good start. Klokker was out, but his place was taken by a tall, burly Dutchman named Daan van Bunge, who had already given a compelling performance for Holland against Warwickshire in the 2005 C&G Trophy, and had batted through Holland's innings against India in the World Cup in South Africa in 2003. It did not take Bunge long to impress himself on the game. Graveney admired his power, and Ted Dexter, who looked in from a holiday he was taking nearby, remarked on how good van Bunge looked. What's his motive in playing for MCC Young Cricketers? 'He wants to become a first-class cricketer. He's desperate to play county cricket,' said Radley.

Radley had mislaid his clever Bangladeshi left-arm spin bowler, Nadif Chowdhary, who had missed the team bus in London, and whose command of English was insufficient to cope with railway timetables. Radley ran an international squad. Besides the Dane and the Dutchman, there was a second Bangladeshi, and 'two Paddies and two Jocks'. (This is Radley blunt-speak.) Nine in all, out of a squad of 20. Just as well that a dispensation had allowed MCC to field two overseas players in their XIs during the campaign.

The squad lived together in a hostel in Hampstead, and each received £200 a week from MCC. 'They have it a lot easier than the boys on the

Clive Radley in his domain: the Indoor School.

old ground staff. It's more like a professional cricketer's life.' Living together 24 hours a day, especially if they were away from home for the first time, was a test of character. 'They have to grow up very quickly,' says Radley. At lunch, Stuart Barnes, who runs Gloucestershire's academy, whose students range from twelve to eighteen and live at home, said how he admired the breadth of the cricket education received at Lord's.

This three-day game went well for MCC, who had taken nine Gloucestershire second-innings wicket with an hour still to play, and confidently expected to win when they were thwarted by rain. Rain ruined more games in August and early September. At the end of the 2nd XI Championship, MCC had won one game (against Durham), lost two (Essex was the other county to beat them), and drawn six of ten games. One had been abandoned. The competition has an incomprehensible points system because not all sides play each other, but they were placed twelfth out of nineteen teams. 'I was worried that they might be stretched too far, but the boys competed pretty well. They all chipped in,' said Radley.

Klokker, who preferred to play for the YCs when he had been selected by Denmark, had attracted interest from Warwickshire and Durham. ('Such a good attitude,' said Radley's end-of-season report.) One of the Jocks – Gordon Gourdie from Aberdeen – had been signed up by Middlesex. A couple more hopefuls might end up with Nottinghamshire and Gloucestershire. Kevin O'Brien, one the Paddies, was anxious to play for Ireland now they had qualified for the 2007 World Cup finals. Back in Bangladesh, the national coach Dav Whatmore had plans for Chowdhary.

The name missing from this list was that of van Bunge. He was the team's top scorer, and had an average in the high 40s. At the end of the season, however, he was in the dumps. Despite his international qualifications, he had not received an offer. Radley thought that perhaps he had not done the business in county trials, but van Bunge was still determined and went on trialling. It would be surprising if nothing turned up for him.

Radley regretted that Caroline Atkins would not be returning to Lord's. MCC Young Women Cricketers work apart from the men. 'The girls mainly do their own thing,' he says. They turn out regularly for MCC women, but the emphasis in their summer is on coaching and training. Atkins, at 24 the oldest of the Young Cricketers, was on the fringe of the England squad, but most women cricketers also need a job. Atkins was going to Bournemouth University as a physical-education coach, having established that her new employers would let her play cricket to her heart's content. She had enjoyed herself at Lord's. 'I'd recommend the Young Cricketers to any aspiring cricketer. It's a great lifestyle.'

Although the Cricket Committee were happy with the team's performances, Tony Lewis and Robin Marlar were pondering ways in which MCC Young Cricketers might be integrated into MCC Universities. Radley, who had clucked over his charges all summer, wondered whether some promising young cricketers who were none too bright academically might no longer qualify. By the end of the season, Radley, feeling knackered and looking forward to a rest, was no less fond of his chicks. 'I like that age group. They're a super bunch, and it's a good education,' he says. 'They keep me young I think.' Radley has the face of a comfortable old boot, but he also has a good heart.

WAITING FOR THE WOMEN

Rachael Heyhoe Flint, who played in goal for England women's hockey team, is a jolly sort. She also captained England women's cricket team. 'In Swanton's phrase, I'm a sort of a cricket person.' Until 1998, however, she was not the sort of person who was allowed to join MCC. She was the wrong sex. She was also the sort of person who thought the exclusion of women was wrong.

Her campaign to end the bar began in 1990. A reporter from the *Daily Mail* had asked if it was true that she was the only woman who was permitted to sit in the Pavilion. It was not true, she replied. No women were allowed to sit in the Pavilion, with the exception of the Queen. 'The man from the *Mail* was shocked,' she recalls. He asked why I didn't try to do something about it. 'Sounds like fun,' she thought at the time.

She was nominated under the name 'R. Flint'. Her sponsors were Sir Tim Rice, Brian Johnston of Test Match Special, Dennis Amiss, the fine Warwickshire and England batsman, and Sir 'Union Jack' Hayward, whose £75,000 donation to club funds in 1976 had allowed MCC to build its new indoor school. 'Not a bad top four in the order' she says. MCC put two and two together. The President, the judge Lord Griffiths, telephoned her personally to say that MCC had never had a membership proposal for a woman. She persisted. It was a hard slog, but she kept her cool. 'You can't be militant when it's a question of changing a constitution that's been around for 204 years.'

Seven more years went by before the vote among MCC members finally went in favour of women members. When the result was announced, her supporters rushed to Lord's Tavern, where she was waiting. She was happy, but she did not linger. A matter-of-fact person, she explained that she was driving home to the Midlands, and she had to be at Sainsbury's first thing the next morning.

Within a few years, she was a fixture at Lord's. As a member of the MCC Committee and two sub-committees she had found a role within the male establishment of MCC and became a trusted advisor, not just on women's cricket.

One reason for her success was that she obviously failed to conform to the stereotype of women cricketers, but she also disarmed the men by her complicit nature. 'I'm not one of the feminist brigade that wants to change Third Man to Third Person Singular.'

At last! Rachael Heyhoe Flint, former England Women's captain, shows off her Member's pass. She led the first group of women who were elected to membership of MCC.

MCC soon organised a women's section to play out-matches, just like the men. In 2005, MCC women played 20 matches plus a few festival games. The big one was against Australia, which was one of only two they lost. The armed services were good for three games. Universities, schools and the odd county filled out the fixture list. MCC does not belong to a league, and the standard ranges from international to good-natured club. 'Some of our opponents, such as Loughborough UCCE, Surrey and Middlesex, are competitive; and some games are played to spread the spirit of cricket,' says Caroline Atkins, a recruit from MCC Young Cricketers.

One of the games was against a team from the Civil Service on Dukes Meadows in Chiswick. This was cricket for the love of it. No casual spectators strolled by as they walked the dog. The only male spectators were the scorer, and me. Civil Service batted first. MCC took the field one short, but were strengthened by Atkins and Laura Joyce, another Young Cricketer. Atkins, a good batsman – she made 50 against Australia – who can bowl a bit, kept wicket, and Joyce, who 'keeps for England 'A', decided she would like to bowl.

MCC's captain was Keely Juster, a schoolteacher, taking advantage of school holidays. She is an accomplished player, captain of Middlesex and the women's team at Gunnersbury, her north London club. Why cricket? She started to play in the garden with her brother, and pestered her father to take her with him when he played club cricket at weekends.

Why MCC? 'The honour, perhaps.' Juster had heard about MCC Women through word of mouth on the fairly limited women's cricket circuit. She was proposed and seconded; as a probationer, she played in five games in two years, notably fewer than the men. She became a member in 2004, in the special class of 'out-match member'. Unlike some of the men, the women appear to carry no social baggage. Most of the players know each other. 'No one thinks MCC is toffee-nosed,' she says.

The men who play in out-matches seem to find it easier to take days off work than women do. None of Juster's team was her own boss, and employers may be less sympathetic towards women who ask for time off to play cricket. MCC had to borrow a fielder for the Civil Service's innings. Civil Service seemed to be on their way to a par score of 190 in 50 overs, thanks largely to a hard-hitting innings by a player who belongs to MCC, but were all out for 168. 'Cricket's a funny old game, and, fortunately, the ball did a bit for us,' says Juster, demonstrating a command of cricket clichés that knows no sexual boundaries.

Caroline Atkins, opening the batting for MCC, was happy to be at the crease. She wanted to work on her paddle sweep, and to hit the ball over the bowler's head earlier than she normally does. She had been on the fringe of the England squad in 2002, before she lost form. When the chance to become a Young Cricketer presented itself, she seized it. 'I couldn't see anything wrong with training from Monday to Friday, and playing a few games.' She played ten for MCC during the summer.

Her father was a cricket coach at Burgess Hill in Sussex. When he registered her enthusiasm and talent – she played with a hard ball from the age of nine – he set up a cricket team at her school to get her some proper matches. Against the Civil Service, she was 79 not out when MCC won, with only two wickets down and ten overs to spare. Another win in a season that had gone well for MCC women; nine games were won, two lost – to Horsham Ladies as well as Australia – three drawn and the rest abandoned. MCC Women's cricket looked healthy enough on Dukes Meadows.

This is not the case. It has not been the success that MCC had hoped for. In 2004, there were only five candidates for playing membership. In the first nine months of 2005, there had been none at all. An inquiry was ordered by the Cricket Committee into this state of affairs, and Heyhoe Flint was asked to get it under way.

She already understood the fundamental problem. There are two streams of women who might be interested in MCC. Women who like watching cricket at Lord's make up one: thousands of them are to be seen at big games, but their interest rarely translates into a membership proposal. 'Lots of them say "what's the point of eighteen years on the waiting list?" '

The second stream comprises the women who play cricket for MCC, and there are not enough of them. They are different from the men, who play because they want to join MCC. Most women play because they enjoy playing, not because they want to join a predominantly male club. Some of those who might wish to join cannot afford to. Heyhoe Flint understands that, if women will not come to MCC, then MCC must reach out to women cricketers, among those who play the game at university, for example. If this means a publicity campaign, then let it commence. For a start it might emphasise that out-match membership is not expensive – the cost is only £37 a year.

A new start would be made. The chairman of the women's cricket sub-committee, Norma Izzard, announced that she was happy to step down. Heyhoe Flint was back on the campaign trail. 'The impact of women's membership has been disappointingly slow,' she says. 'Throughout the campaign, I stressed that we didn't want any favours, but we've only got 358 members.' After fighting for 30 years to have women's cricket fully integrated into the community of cricket, the last thing she wants is for women to become a satellite body on the fringe of MCC.

THE GROUNDSMAN'S SEASON

BEHIND THE SCENES: '*Saturday 2nd July 2005 – It's the Natwest Series Final between England and Australia and the atmosphere is palpable in the packed ground. It's mean out there on the pitch today, as the tractors and rollers take cover behind the gate and in the shadow of the protective Media Centre. Poor Trescothick has to duck a beamer from the Australian bowler (I think it was McGrath). And the excitement continued right until the last ball and amazingly and rarely, the two teams had to share the prize – should be a very exciting next few weeks…*'

Cricket at Lord's in the summer of 2005 ended late in the afternoon of 11 September. Scott Styris of Middlesex bowled Glamorgan's Dean Cosker to win a National League game by 5 runs. That same evening, Mick Hunt, the groundsman, was watering the whole of the square as a preliminary to getting down to serious work on the following morning. He had to hurry. The next Test against Sri Lanka was precisely eight months away. Hunt's window of opportunity was narrower than he would like.

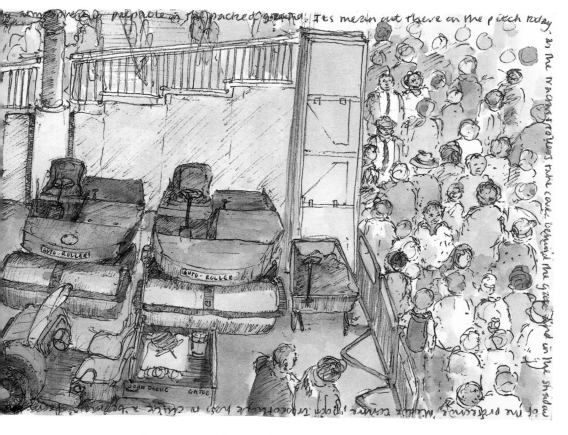

After five months' heavy duty in 2005, the square was exhausted. There had been two Tests, two ODIs, seven four-day county matches, and 21 miscellaneous one-day matches. The Lord's wicket had played well during the summer. Hunt recalled that, when seventeen wickets fell on the first day of the Ashes Test, some former Test players who ought to know better had expressed doubts about the pitch. Hunt was proud of the way it had played, with plenty of movement at the start, and good carry through to the 'keeper, proof of a quick wicket. 'A lot of players were caught out because it was that quick,' says Hunt. He reports that both umpires had marked the pitch 'good'. Justin Langer called it a fine Test wicket. Hunt rested his case.

There had been a heavy price to pay. According to Hunt: 'Pitches this year were the barest I've seen them for some time.' The reason, he said, was 'a ridiculously overloaded programme at Lord's.' It is the groundsman's familiar lament. Because the cricket season starts so early, Hunt has to be ready to take full advantage of the autumn growing season. The day after the Middlesex game, he and his crew were on the square with the scarifier, which pulls out any shallow-rooting grass. Then he top dresses each pitch with a mixture of clay and sand. He sows rye grass where the patches require it. 'If you get it right in September, you get it right for the next year.'

Hunt's constant fear is the weather. Having started work on the day England won the Ashes, he was hard at it the following day – a fine one in which he was able to strip down to his shorts, though he did put his shirt back on for the arrival of the England team. After three days, just as the rain began to fall, they had only four pitches to go. 'We worked ourselves into the ground.'

He worries because of the unpredictable mixture of sun and rain in September. Some rain is good; too much is disastrous. Because of the slope, heavy rain washes the top dressing and the grass seed down towards the Tavern Stand. At worst, the square is left bare of its new goodness, and the outfield becomes a quagmire. 'You're on a wing and a prayer with preparation,' says Hunt.

Hunt's other concern during the summer had been the drop-in pitches, growing in a far corner of the Nursery Ground. As a groundsman, he understands the case for them. Used pitches are hard to repair when they are in the middle of the playing area. When they are resting in the Nursery Ground, they can be worked on while a game is being played. Drop-in pitches are at the experimental stage, and Hunt remains non-committal about them.

At the end of another season – his 37th at Lord's – his preoccupation was with the future. But his future is the start of a new cricket season. At the beginning of April 2006, Hunt's poor, battered, beautifully green square comes back as host to 'far too much cricket'.

GOOD REVIEWS

The last Executive Board meeting of Tom Graveney's Presidential year took place amid euphoria, the day after England won the Ashes. But it was business as usual; improvements to the real tennis court were discussed, and thought was given to ways of getting kids to play cricket in public parks. Eventually, Charles Fry the Chairman said a formal farewell to the President. Choosing Graveney as his successor, he said, was the best decision he had ever made. For his part, Graveney said what a great honour it had been, and thanked them for thanking him.

Stephanie Lawrence, who had looked after Graveney's diary for the year, recorded the exchange in the minutes. She has worked at Lord's since 1968 and she describes the transformation of MCC through the people she had worked with. S. C. Griffith was a club man ('he'd be floundering now') working behind the scenes with 'Gubby' Allen ('not my favourite man'). Then came Jack Bailey ('very single-minded; the members didn't appreciate that'); next was Col. Stephenson ('we were his troops, and loved it'), and finally Roger Knight ('he loves new things; he's been very innovative').

Despite having watched MCC change over nearly four decades, she was still surprised by Graveney's nomination as President. 'We've not gone down the path of professional cricketers before. It's usually a committee man. I was absolutely delighted.' She had got to know him soon after she arrived at Lord's, and thought of him as a cricketer of the old school, along with the likes of Compton, Edrich, Parfitt and Titmus. Those players had become friendly with the staff; they would drink together in the old Tavern. Graveney was a regular visitor on major match days, when he took over from Peter May the role played by former England cricketers of host in one of the private boxes. May had hosted a box for the insurers Willis Faber. Having succeeded May, Graveney enjoyed the company, returning every year kept him in touch with Lord's. Speaking of that generation, Lawrence added, 'You'd never pass one of them on the stairs without stopping for a chat. If an England player now said "good morning", I think I'd have a fit.'

She had been at most of the committee meetings Graveney had attended. 'He didn't say a lot,' she reports, 'but he's sharp. He doesn't get drawn into the waffle. He's a stickler, good on detail. It's a shame to lose him – you need the pertinent remark. He's a valuable cricket voice too.' But Lawrence thought his greatest value was outside the committee rooms. 'Wherever Tom's gone this year, MCC has perched on his shoulder. He became synonymous with MCC.'

Lord's is at the bottom of Colin Ingleby-Mackenzie's back garden. As a trustee, he is an ebullient presence. When he retired from playing county cricket, he became someone in the City. He was nominated President himself in 1996/98, and pushed through the election of women, often shooting from the hip. Bob Alexander, the grand QC and eminent banker, would sit next to Ingleby-Mackenzie, slipping him notes suggesting that sometimes it is better to let your opponents talk themselves out: 'a very subtle piece of advice'.

Ingleby-Mackenzie had played against Graveney when he was captain of Hampshire, and recalled that some of his fellow professionals thought Graveney a little selfish. 'He wasn't Mr Popular with everybody, but he did everything to help me, and he was a hell of a player.' Ingleby-Mackenzie recalls a tour of the West Indies during which he shared a room in Bridgetown with J. J. Warr, the Middlesex fast bowler. Warr was night-watchman, with Graveney due in to bat next. Room service was provided by a man named Martindale, and Ingleby-Mackenzie decided it would be a good idea to ask Martindale if he had any advice to Warr about playing the West Indies fast bowlers. 'That's easy,' said Martindale. 'Tell him to slog out and make way for Mr Tom.'

Charles Fry had asked Ingleby-Mackenzie for advice about the succession. Casting his mind back over the various members who had done the job in the last few years, he said that his role had been to force the pace. Of the other recent incumbents, Bob Alexander wanted to professionalise the administration, Ted Dexter hoped to encourage cricket and Sir Tim Rice was a fan. Ingleby-Mackenzie's advice was unequivocal. 'I said it was time to have somebody different – not of the people exactly, but a great cricketer. There was nobody better in an Australian year than Graveney. He does not dance on table tops. There's not a lot of the splash of the soda siphon. He's still quietly and beautifully mannered. Absolutely right for this particular year. As far as I'm concerned, he hasn't put a foot wrong.'

Fry confirmed that a number of people had said to him that Graveney was the best choice he had ever made. But why? The timing had been right.

David Batts, Michael Atherton and Colin Ingleby-Mackenzie, a former MCC President, discuss the portrait of Shane Warne.

'In the President's Box during the Ashes Test, Tom was wonderful because he had played with all the old Australian players. Being entertained by him made them really feel at home.'

Fry had become a connoisseur of Graveney's short speeches. 'They were the work of an inspiring figure who transparently loves the game, its ethos and its spirit.' Fry is an English figure: straight, tall and not given to extravagant expressions of feeling. But Graveney seems to have inspired them in him. 'As a cricketer, Tom is a sort of god for a person my age. As President, that helps; but it is no use being a god if you upset people and they don't like you. I've yet to meet anyone who does not think that Tom is the loveliest human being. What better person to be President of MCC than one who starts by being a god, and who is in love with the game of cricket?'

Tom Graveney left the Committee Room as President for the last time, and skirted the Long Room where tables were being laid for the end-of-season staff lunch, at which he would make a short speech. His speaking style, so admired by Fry, comes about as a consequence of worrying beforehand and relaxing in delivery. 'When I get up in front of people, I just look at the ground I'm in and go back to what has happened there.' He had been involved with the administration of Lord's only when he was up in front of the beak in 1962 and 1969. Now, he was an admirer of the efficiency and friendliness of the staff, and he would tell them so.

Dressed in the same light-grey suit and the red-and-yellow club tie he had worn when we met the previous October, he declared that he had not put on any weight, despite all the entertaining at lunches and dinners, 'Touch wood, my health has lasted into my 79th year. I've always looked after myself.' As a player, he had drunk a fair amount of beer. 'But I always had a net in the morning, to shake up my liver and keep fit.' Perhaps, but he was looking weary now, and he was anxious to get back to his wife Jackie in Cheltenham. 'It's easy for me, talking among cricketers. She was nervous about this to begin with, but it got better and better, and she's enjoyed it. My daughter Becky, who also helped me a lot, is a natural.'

At the end of his Presidential year, he did have some regrets. Although he

VIEW FROM THE MOUND STAND: *'Saturday May 28th 2005 – Third day of England v. Bangladesh – the sun is out there – but up here in the Mound Stand (or as I think of it the Hopkins Stand – as I came to see this architectural masterpiece back in 1989 as an architectural student) the wind has cleverly funnelled all of its energy in this direction, so the thermos flask is a necessity. I've only got going with this sketch and it's all over – Bangladesh is out and England has won, and it's only lunchtime. Oh well I hope they will let me back into this box to finish my sketch…yes they did on Saturday June 18th for the Eton v. Harrow match – not as crowded, but probably much louder…'*

felt it was impossible to get to the whole range of MCC's activities in only twelve months, he felt he had neglected some of it. However, it was not ignoring the Arts and Library Committee, or the Laws Working Party, that he really regretted. 'I should have tried to play a bit of golf for MCC,' he said,. 'I feel guilty about missing out on that, but my knee is not great.

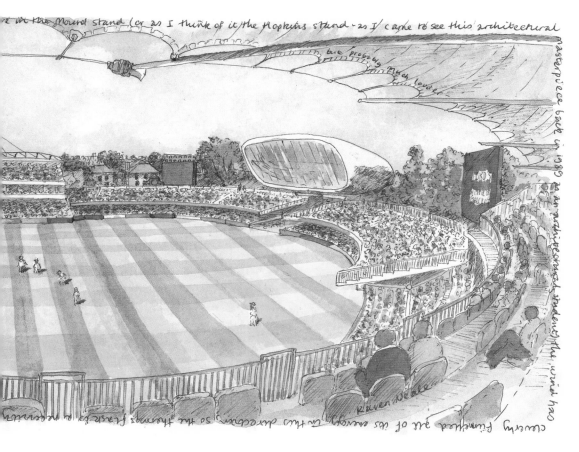

I might be able to make up for it if my knee gets better. Play in a couple of matches for them, just to get to know them.'

When we first talked, he had said his priority was to get more youngsters playing cricket. He was particularly anxious that the Chance to Shine campaign should be well supported. The idea is to persuade many more kids in state schools to play cricket. The campaign intends to raise millions of pounds from private sources, in the expectation that the government will provide matching funding. But MCC has seemed lukewarm about this during Graveney's term. Graveney explains loyally that the golden rule is that MCC should always be able to see where its money is going. 'We must remember it's not our money; the money belongs to the members.'

Chance to Shine initially identified a dozen or so centres from which to conduct the campaign. 'We want to see them, to judge whether our money would be well spent.' He personally would continue to support the campaign after his term ended, he said. He had recently been invited to a game between the Houses of Lords and Commons and an Indian Parliament XI, and had come away with a cheque for £5,000 for Chance to Shine.

As he was about to leave Lord's, he said he suspected he would not be able to stay away. He is likely to host the Willis box again in 2006, despite the danger that it will be an anti-climax. 'I still can't believe I was President. It was something out of the blue. Marvellous, marvellous. It's a year I'll never forget.' Nor will any fan of English cricket, because 2005 was the year England regained the Ashes.

Michael Vaughan and the real Ashes urn. He formally returned the replica and the other Ashes trophies to Lord's after England had paraded them through central London.

THE ASHES REGAINED

At the Oval on 12 September, after the drawn Test that gave England a 2 to 1 series victory, Graveney presented Michael Vaughan with the crystal glass trophy shaped like the original urn – the substitute that has been presented to the winner since 1999. 'That wasn't a bad thing to be able to do,' he said afterwards, pushing understatement as far as it will go. A replica of the urn, kept in a drawer in Adam Chadwick's office and used for photo-shoots and dinners, had been supplied by MCC. That was a better icon than a Waterford glass vase. In the most striking photographic image of the day, Vaughan pressed the replica urn to his lips. He threw it to Flintoff, and it was drowned in champagne. Even though this was not the real thing, Chadwick, watching on TV, fretted about the damage that might be done to it.

The Ashes series was chaos at the end. No one was sure about the script for such a momentous event. Out of the confusion, Vaughan emerged with two trophies – the crystal replica and the trophy donated by npower, the series sponsor. The new Compton/Miller medal for the Man of the Series – named after two of the greatest of Ashes cricketers – was awarded to Andrew Flintoff, a beaming giant. Graveney thought justice would have been better served if Flintoff had shared the medal with Shane Warne. 'He was absolutely fantastic, the way he carried such a massive load on his shoulders.'

Being at the Oval at the climax of such a series vividly recalled 1953 for Graveney, when England had regained the Ashes after a twenty-year gap.

This time, more than eighteen years had passed since a series victory over Australia, and the moment seemed, if anything, to be even sweeter. This time, the celebration had been more choreographed. When Denis Compton hit the winning runs in 1953, the ground was invaded. In 2005, a heavy presence of stewards and police prevented any incursions. 'In my day, the crowd was solid in front of the Pavilion. All the way out to the square was solid with people, and I can see Len [Hutton] holding the urn on the balcony now,' says Graveney.

His memory of that historic series remains fresh. Bad weather meant that neither side had won a Test before the Oval. 'I think perhaps we were ahead on points' – but he also remembered a dropped catch that delayed England's victory celebration. 'I was at short extra cover, saving us a single. Ray Lindwall went to hit either Lockie [Tony Lock] or [Jim] Laker, and he sliced it. Alec Bedser was at deep mid-off, but he didn't seem to want it, so I ended up coming round trying to catch it. I dropped it, and Ray got 60-odd. And I only got 4 with the bat.' It was his first Ashes series, and England won comfortably in the end. Time for a drink, surely, and some exuberant celebration? Not at all. Graveney was scheduled to play for Gloucestershire the next day. Jackie was waiting for him in the car park, ready for a quick getaway.

In 2005, the drama was, if anything, more intense; certainly more unremitting. 'It's been the most fascinating series I've ever come across. Every day of every Test, there's been some enormous performance. If anyone wrote a book about it, no one would believe it.' Like everyone who saw the photograph of Flintoff consoling Brett Lee after Australia's 2-run defeat at Edgbaston, Graveney admired this show of sportsmanship and decency. 'That's what the game's all about.'

He recalled some poor umpiring decisions: 'We all need a bit of luck to win.' Graveney thought England nearly choked at Trent Bridge; but Ricky Ponting got no sympathy for his complaint about being run out by a substitute in the fourth Test at Trent Bridge. 'It was a bloody awful run.' Overall, England were the better side throughout the contest, he said.

'We've got a young side that will go on for another five years. Cricket is booming. We must make sure we take advantage of it.' His first chance to do so came the following day.

The Ashes, in their tiny, irreplaceable urn, belong in the Museum at Lord's. For years, cracks in the shoulders and the stem of the urn have meant it is not allowed to travel; and each time they won an Ashes series, the Australians complained that they were not able to hold the trophy they had won. But it had been repaired by conservation specialists at Plowden & Smith, and on the day before the Oval Test, MCC announced that it will go to Australia during the next Ashes series in 2006/07. Negotiations were underway with Virgin Atlantic Airlines and its Australian subsidiary, Virgin Blue. (It will fly Upper Class, promised Richard Branson, Virgin's Chairman.) The plan was to exhibit the urn in a number of Australian cities. It is fine irony that when it actually gets there, the Ashes will be held by England.

This token of Anglo-Australian relations is still fragile enough to disturb Chadwick's subconscious. During the Oval Test, he dreamed that he had taken the original urn to a match to show to an Australian friend. And the Australian dropped it. No psychoanalyst was needed to interpret that nightmare.

On the day after the final Test, the crystal trophy and npower's series trophy were to come home to join the urn at the Home of Cricket. After the open-top bus parade through the City, the celebration in Trafalgar Square, and the visit to 10 Downing Street, 'closure' – jargon word – would be achieved at Lord's.

Tuesday was already a busy day at Lord's. On a bright, cloudless morning, Cross Arrows were playing on the Nursery Ground. Mick Hunt and his team were busy on the square, and the caterers were preparing the Long Room for the staff lunch. That would be cleared away promptly so that it could be transformed for a reception, provided by Vodafone, the team sponsors.

The arrival of the England team was not to be as public occasion, though MCC members would, of course, be allowed into their club. Parties of schoolchildren who had been left out at the Oval were seated at the front

What the fuss is about. The Ashes urn commemorates England's defeat by Australia at the Oval in 1882. During its recent restoration, MCC were asked if they would like an analysis of the contents. The offer was declined.

of the Pavilion. TV cameras and still photographers set up their pitches on the outfield. The children, who had been given small replica bats, clamoured for autographs from anyone who looked distinguished and was willing to sign. Tom Graveney became a name on their little bats. One day, they may discover who he was.

The England team arrived at the Nursery End in mid-afternoon, neatly dressed in dark blazers and team ties. The groundsmen retired to the lee of the Grand Stand. The players, who would have understood that there was no short-cut across the square, were shepherded around it. When they arrived in front of the Pavilion, the children shrieked; adults applauded warmly. Our heroes, many of them wearing dark glasses, signed the children's bats. Kevin Pietersen's 158 the day before had been the most important innings by an England batsman since his fellow South African Basil D'Oliviera scored exactly the same number of runs against Australia in 1968. Now he towered over the children, showing the thick white stripe in his hair as he leant over to sign his name.

A formal team photograph was taken of both men's and women's England teams. The women had also just beaten the Australians themselves. The crystal vase and the npower trophy were placed on a side table. Vaughan drifted over and formally handed them to Graveney for safe keeping. He clutched both in his arms before passing them on to Chadwick, who took them to their new home.

Players and spectators filed into the Long Room, where champagne was served. Lord MacLaurin, chairman of Vodafone, who was the host, was saying to all and sundry that he had laid the foundation when he was chairman of the ECB. True enough: both central contracts and Duncan Fletcher had arrived on his watch. The players mingled with staff from MCC and the ECB, and with journalists. After nearly 24 hours of celebration, some of them were not making much sense. Matthew Hoggard was being nice to the girls, many of whom were intent on getting England shirts signed by the whole team. Flintoff exuded bleary bonhomie, and called for more beer. Vaughan looked tired and fulfilled. Pietersen looked for some action.

Fletcher, who had been granted British citizenship that morning – years after his original application – made a short speech that was entirely to the point: 'I hadn't realised the enormity of the passion to beat Australia among England's players and it has surprised me that we have beaten them so soon.'

Graveney slipped away after learning that he was not required to speak. He felt very tired now, and Jackie was waiting for him in Cheltenham. 2005 had been the most historic year in English cricket since 1953, and Tom Graveney had left a mark on both, first as the most elegant of England's best batsmen, and, 52 years on, as a graceful President of MCC. Not at all a bad thing to be able to do.

INDEX